INCREDIBLE
OPTICAL ILLUSIONS

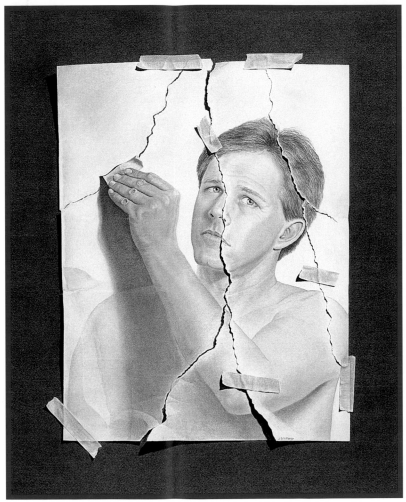

IDENTICAL IMAGES?

Our eye leaps to the assumption that these two photographs are identical. But it is an illusion. Look again to see if you can spot the differences, and turn to pages 122-3 to see how you have done.

INCREDIBLE
OPTICAL ILLUSIONS

A spectacular journey
through the world
of the impossible

NIGEL RODGERS

CONSULTANT EDITOR: DR IAN GORDON

BARNES
&NOBLE

BOOKS
NEW YORK

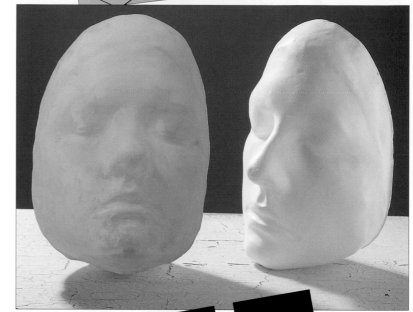

This edition published by
Barnes & Noble, Inc.,
by arrangement with Quarto Inc.
1998 Barnes & Noble Books

ISBN 0-7607-0800-2

This book was designed and produced by
Quarto Publishing plc
6 Blundell Street
London N7 9BH

Library of Congress Cataloging Data available upon
request.

ISBN 0-7607-0800-2

Project Editor *Rebecca Moy*
Editor *John Farndon*
Editorial Director *Gilly Cameron Cooper*
Designer *Frances de Rees*
Art Editor *Elizabeth Healey*
Assistant Art Director *Penny Cobb*
Picture Researchers *Miriam Hyman,*
Gill Metcalfe, Steven Lai
Photographers *Paul Forrester, David Kemp*
Illustrators *Kevin Maddison, Janos Marffy,*
John Blackman, David Kemp, Neil Bullpit
Art Director *Moira Clinch*

Manufactured in Hong Kong by
Regent Publishing Services Ltd
Printed in China by Leefung-Asco
Printers Ltd

CONTENTS

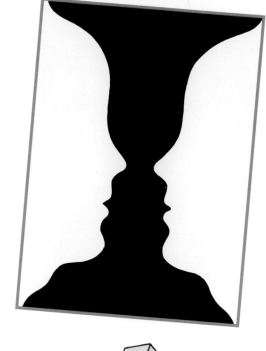

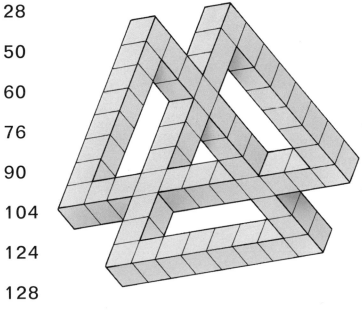

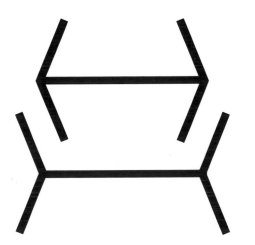

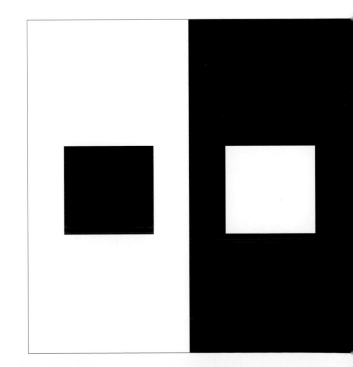

INTRODUCTION

YOU SHOULD NEVER BELIEVE YOUR EYES...

...Not, that is, if you expect them to tell you the whole truth and nothing but the truth about the world around you. What you think you are seeing is really only a slice, a section of the world—inevitably, for you are bombarded with so much information by your eyes that your mind has to filter out and to arrange in order of importance what you finally "see". If you did not do this, you could not live. To take a simple example: a cat close up looks larger than a truck a mile away. You know, intellectually, that the truck is far bigger so this does not upset you but, if you worked on the assumption that the cat really was bigger than a truck, you could be in trouble.

Our whole world is made of such visual illusions. If you look at the moon rising or setting on the horizon, it will appear far larger than when it is high in the sky. Nearly two thousand years ago the Ancient Greek astronomer Ptolemy noted this phenomenon and realized that what caused it was not a change in the nature of the moon itself, nor even of light, but in the way human beings perceive it. Even today, however, scientists still cannot explain exactly how this happens. If you look in a mirror, you will see your perfectly reproduced image—but one which is reversed, from left to right, and smaller than you are. The farther you move from the mirror, the smaller you will look, for you are doubly distant. But your brain automatically compensates for this reversal and diminution.

If you look at a picture, whether a painting, photograph, movie, or television image, what you are seeing is a two-dimensional surface. But what you imagine you see is a three-dimensional view stretching in from the picture plane, as in the painting below. This stunning illusion of depth is based on lines arrowing in to the vanishing point—the point where seemingly parallel lines inside the picture meet. The laws of scientific or linear perspective were invented in the Renaissance in the 1400s as the definitive way of reproducing the three-dimensional world on a two-dimensional surface.

When photography developed in the mid 1800s, it was regarded as completely objective. The camera never lies, it was said. We know

Our senses do not deceive us. This is not because they always judge correctly, but because they do not judge at all.

Immanuel Kant

Piero della Francesca
THE ANNUNCIATION
Your eye rushes in down the long rows of columns (*below*) to the wall at the end. All is seemingly so solid and so three-dimensional that it is impossible not to accept the illusion of real depth and space.

6

better now, aware that the camera can deceive in all sorts of ways, but it is still hard to realize how artificial and selective it actually is. Shown early monochrome photographs, many people in rural Africa failed to recognize their villages or even themselves from the surfaces. Uninfluenced by Western culture, they did not fall for the illusion of depth. Instead, they often preferred drawings showing elephants, for example, as larger than antelopes even when they were farther away. Small children also paint happily disregarding not only linear perspective but also foreshortening, another trick used by Western artists. Today it is realized there is nothing childish about such approaches. But it suggests that many common preconceptions about how you view the world are, at least in part, shared illusions, dependant on your particular cultural background.

ILLUSIONS NOT DELUSIONS

If you have a high fever or are taking drugs or the balance of your mind is otherwise disturbed, you may suffer hallucinations or other visual delusions. Alarmingly convincing though they may be, they are entirely subjective and cannot be photographed. By contrast, optical illusions not only can be photographed, but often work better when seen through a camera. Impossible figures such as those pioneered by Roger Penrose (*see pp.64-5*) make good sense to the eye and look even more convincing in a photograph, but are rejected by the mind as utterly impossible. Such impossibilities, which are only just impossible, tease our Western sense of perspective, raising questions of how far what we see is what we are conditioned to see.

Optical illusions remain at the frontier of our understanding of the mind's workings. The eye itself is a minor miracle, processing constant and massive light stimuli into meaningful information.

INSIDE THE EYE

The human eye in some ways resembles a very specialized camera, for its lens is adjusted by the eye's shape being constantly changed by muscles inside the eyeball. The lens projects a reversed, inverted and reduced image of the outer world onto the retina, which is a network of some 200 million light-sensitive cells called photoreceptors.

This remarkably complex and sensitive organ connects so intimately with the mind that, for practical non-specialist purposes, the dividing line between mind and eye is often blurred. You can talk of the brain and eye almost as a continuum. It has been shown that changing mental attitudes to seeing can improve poor or damaged eyesight in at least some cases.

Your mind and eye work together, trying to make sense of the incomplete or ambiguous. Optical illusions, by their very nature, tend to be ambiguous and are often incomplete—until the mind and eye complete them according to what they expect or hope to see in the world.

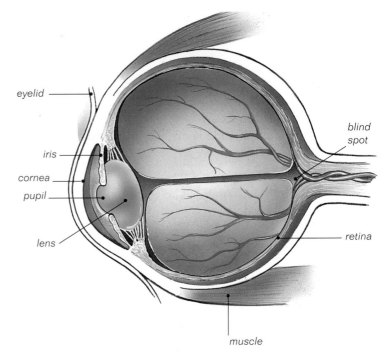

eyelid

iris

cornea

pupil

lens

blind spot

retina

muscle

inverted, reduced and reversed image projected onto the retina.

CHAPTER 1

PERSPECTIVE

So convincingly three-dimensional is the picture on the left that you perceive it in exactly the same way as a view through a window, with real depth and space. You could confidently assert that the columns are in the foreground, fairly nearby. The round temple rotunda you might judge to be further away, no more than 40 yards or so. The trees, perhaps, are 150 yards away. And the sea may perhaps be 600 yards away. Yet this is all an illusion. The column, the rotunda, the tree and the sea are all exactly the same distance away—they are, of course, all on the surface of this page. This is the illusion of perspective, the trick of creating the look of the third dimension on a two-dimensional surface. From this fundamental optical illusion—which has been an essential element of Western art for nearly 600 years—many others are derived.

DISCOVERY OF PERSPECTIVE

Look at a simple painting of a landscape. If it seems right and natural—if the houses look solid and the distant hills far away—you are being taken in by an illusion, the illusion of perspective. You know the painting is just a flat surface covered in paint, yet it looks as if it has real depth and space—just like the view through a window or doorway. This impression of depth and space has been a part of Western art for so long that we often take it for granted. But it is a carefully contrived illusion.

EYE OF A NEEDLE

A camel may not hope to pass through the eye of a needle, but its image *(below)*, much reduced through the laws of perspective, can.

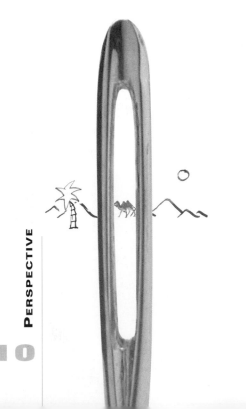

In looking at the world, we accept without thinking that the farther away something is, the smaller it appears. From a skyscraper, the cars below look like toys. A child nearby looks bigger than an adult in the distance. But just because distant things look small, we don't assume that they are small. A variety of clues within the scene tell the brain that they are small only because they are further away. It is these clues which form the basis of perspective.

We learn these clues so thoroughly during early childhood, that they become second nature and we only rarely make mistakes in everyday life. In fact, we can judge fairly accurately how far away someone is simply by how small they appear. But it was a long time before artists around the world began to exploit these perspective clues to create the illusion of depth in their pictures.

In the earliest paintings, the size of figures bears no relation to how far away they are. Often, the biggest figures in a painting are simply the most important. This is so in, for example, both medieval European paintings or Indian Mughal miniatures of the 1600s. The beautifully drawn detail in many of these pictures shows that the artists were competent painters—but if they understood perspective, they had no interest in using it to create an illusion of depth. Often they were painting more with symbolic or even magical meanings. In Japan and China, landscape painters developed a way of painting convincing, beautiful landscapes without reducing distant objects in size. In fact, the Chinese probably were aware of the principle of perspective but regarded it as vulgar and so ignored it.

In the West, some early painters realized intuitively that figures in the background ought to be smaller than those in the foreground. Ancient Greek artists knew about "foreshortening." When you stand close in front of, say, a square house, the sides look much shorter than the front. Similarly, if an arm points directly at you from close to, the hand should look massive and the arm tiny. That the Greeks knew about this is evident from Greek sculpture, especially low-relief. However, they do not seem to have known—or taken an interest in—how to create the entire range of perspective clues.

ARTISTIC LICENSE

Knowledge of the laws of scientific perspective, so important in the West, is not needed to create a convincing representation of reality, as this Indian picture c. 1600 *(right)* demonstrates.

MATHEMATICALLY PERFECT
Accurate perspective is vital to townscape paintings such as this anonymous view of Venice (*above*) in the 1500s. Your eye is drawn past the Piazzetta San Marco into the Piazza San Marco (St. Mark's Square), apparently into a three-dimensional depth, by the mathematically perfect use of single point perspective.

THE DISCOVERY OF LINEAR PERSPECTIVE

In the early 1400s, Italian Renaissance artists, especially in Florence, started trying to represent the world exactly as it was, analyzing it carefully and rationally. Many of these painters were architects too, concerned with practical building problems—such as how their structures would look from a distance. Indeed, it is the architect Filippo Brunelleschi (1377–1446) who is credited by the great architect, sculptor and writer Leon Alberti (1404–72) with discovering true perspective in painting. In a series of panels (now lost), Brunelleschi showed the buildings of Florence exactly as they are, by using for the first time the idea of a single central viewpoint. Beyond this viewpoint everything gets smaller and smaller in the distance and eventually disappears altogether. The result is that lines converge on a single point on the horizon, later called the vanishing point.

A single vanishing point forms the basis of what we now call mathematical, scientific, or linear perspective. This analyzes what appears to happen to lines that stretch away from you into the distance. These lines are at right angles to the picture plane and are called orthogonals. Of course, since these lines are parallel, they never meet. But they give the illusion of doing so at a calculated point on the horizon: the vanishing point. This is the point to which your eye is drawn, although often it is hidden by buildings or mountains. In the early Renaissance, painters

HOW IT WORKS: the vanishing point

FROM A BRIDGE over a straight railroad track, the parallel rails seem to arrow together in the distance, finally appearing to merge at a single point on the horizon known as the vanishing point. This is the point at which all parallel lines seem to meet, but of course it is an illusion; in reality, they are just as far apart at the horizon as they are nearby.

To see how effective it can be to use this illusion in paintings, try drawing a table with all the edges completely parallel. Use a ruler to help you. You will find the table looks very strange. If you now draw the lines converging inwards at the correct angle, they will give the illusion of being parallel as they recede into the picture.

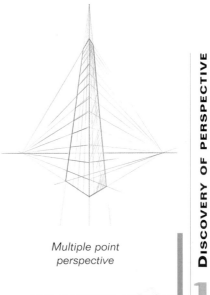

Two point perspective

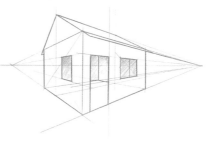

Multiple point perspective

used only one vanishing point, usually right in the center of a picture. This gives a remarkably strong three-dimensional effect, like that in Piero della Francesca's *Annunciation* (*see p. 6*), with all the diagonals arrowing in towards the wall.

In his book *De Pictura* (About Painting), Alberti compares a painting to a window through which we look out onto the world. The great Renaissance artist and thinker Leonardo da Vinci (1452–1519) went further, saying "perspective is nothing more than seeing a place [as if] behind a plane of glass... on the surface of which objects behind the glass are drawn." This implies a scientific rather than visual approach to painting, and Leonardo wanted painting to be regarded as a science. The effect of such an approach can be seen in the anonymous view of Venice above and in a much later painting, *The Piazzetta: Looking North* by the 1700s Venetian master of perspective Canaletto (1697–1768). These paintings seem as objectively convincing as the photographs with which they can be compared for accuracy. But we should never forget that they are illusions.

Impressive as such Renaissance pictures are, we do not always look at the world as if it is focused on a single point. To convey the complexity of the real world better, later artists took to using two or more vanishing points on the horizon when painting particularly hilly landscapes or stormy seascapes. Artists can now learn either of these techniques in a few hours.

VIEWPOINTS AND VANISHING POINTS

When they discovered perspective, the artists of the Renaissance used it in a very particular way. Most pictures of the time are painted as if there is just a single, central point of view, and lines of perspective converge on a single vanishing point.

STEP BY STEP:
Do it yourself. Simple perspective

It took the artists of the 1300s and 1400s generations to work out the principles of perspective. Today, you can learn them simply and swiftly to create the illusion of three-dimensional depth in your pictures. They are based on the convention or illusion that you are viewing the world from a fixed viewpoint as if through a sheet of glass, or a window.

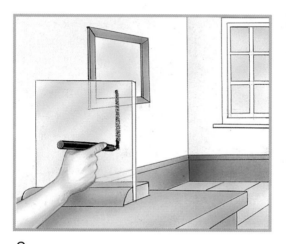

1 Shut one eye and look through a square of glass at your scene. Ideally for this exercise the scene should be a perfectly symmetrical rectangular room, but any relatively regular street or landscape will do.

2 Prop up the glass so that you can draw on it without moving it at all. Then as you look through the glass draw on it with a felt-tip pen all the outlines you see.

3 Now examine all the lines on the glass carefully and compare them with the lines and directions in reality. You will find that when rectangular shapes are flat on to the glass, the outlines are parallel both vertically and horizontally. But if they are at an angle to the glass, the lines converge towards the distance, so that all would ultimately come together at a single point, at eye level or the horizon.

4 Now copy these lines on to a sheet of paper and use them as a model to help you draw or paint the scene. Use a ruler to help confirm the accuracy of your converging lines.

MULTIPLE PERSPECTIVE

The single viewpoint/vanishing point perspective renders the world with a simple but very dignified realism that suited the Renaissance artists to perfection, which is why it is still popular for ceremonial portraits. It was also very easy for novice painters to master. But it is by no means the only kind of perspective. In reality, there is often more than one vanishing point—and more than one point of view. Imagine, for instance, standing at the corner of a house. The lines of the front of the house will have a different vanishing point to the lines of the side of the house. This is two-point perspective. Many scenes have multiple vanishing points. Even in multiple point perspective, the vanishing points must always be at eye level, as the single point in Raphael's picture is. False perspective illusions are created by placing vanishing points at slightly different levels—but so close to eye level that the difference is imperceptible.

Raphael (1483-1520)

THE SCHOOL OF ATHENS

This Italian masterpiece (*right and below*) looks so convincing that it is easy to overlook the fact that its air of three-dimensional reality is based on the concept of the single vanishing point—but the actual world is not quite so restricted.

AMES ROOMS

Every now and then someone finds an ingenious way to exploit our tendency to take the rules of perspective for granted. With a little gentle trickery, the eye can be persuaded into all kinds of mistakes, as Adelbert Ames showed with his strange and remarkable false-perspective rooms.

The rooms where most of us live and work are roughly rectangular, and your view of the world is adjusted to this. If you enter a large room and see a person standing in each of the far corners, you can probably guess which is the taller—but not in a room designed by Adelbert Ames. In an Ames Room, things are not what they seem. By exploiting our expectation that rooms are rectangular, Ames can create weird illusions. Adelbert Ames started life as a painter before turning to perhaps the most famous of all demonstrations of the limitations of linear perspective. He wrote almost nothing about his ideas or motives but made several full-scale models of rooms. If viewed from a particular point, an Ames Room looks quite normal and rectangular. Yet a person standing in one far corner looks like a giant compared to a person in the other.

The explanation for this baffling phenomenon is that the room is not actually rectangular at all. It has been carefully constructed and painted, using misleading perspective clues to give the illusion that it is rectangular. It is in fact, a weird wedge shape, as a different viewpoint clearly reveals. So the giant is only a giant because he is much nearer. The eye is deceived by the way Ames designed the windows and doors of the far wall, which grow larger quite imperceptibly as they slope away to the left. Your eye and brain wrongly assume the opposite wall is flat (as normal) and both figures are at identical distances from you. The only way to discover the true dimensions of the room is to do so by touch, using perhaps a long stick, because the eye (or the brain's interpretation of what the eye sees) remains obstinately deceived.

AMES ROOM

Stand at the entrance (VP) to an Ames Room and you will apparently see a giant on your right (B) and a dwarf on your left (A). Distorted perspectives fool the brain into thinking that the two people are the same distance away from you.

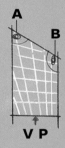

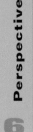

DID YOU KNOW?
The African view
of perspective

INTERESTINGLY, people who have grown up in traditional Africa (*above*) where many houses are round, not rectangular, seem less baffled by Ames Rooms than most Europeans. Presumably their ways of seeing are less preconditioned by straight lines and rectangular forms. On the other hand, the anthropologist Colin Turnbull relates in his book *The Forest People* that African pygmies who have spent their whole lives in a forest are baffled by their first sight of the wider world beyond. Seeing a buffalo grazing a mile away from the forest's edge, a pygmy with Turnbull thought it was a fly, unable to associate the tiny image to a large creature, for his mental eye had never had to cope with such large distances.

HOW IT WORKS: mirror images

DURING CHILDHOOD, we learn to interpret clues to distance and size so well that we can easily forget they are just clues—and may be misleading. One way to show this is to look at yourself in a normal mirror at the normal distance. Then measure the outline of your face on the mirror using toothpaste or shaving foam. You will be amazed at how much smaller the outline of your face is. Do the same with a full-length mirror and you will find that if you are a person of normal height, your image in the mirror is just 3 feet (90 cm) tall. Double the normal distance you stand from the mirror and you will approximately halve the size of your image—yet you still are your normal height.

PERFECT BUILDINGS

Many of the greatest and most inspiring Western buildings look perfectly, even sublimely, four-square and rectangular in their proportions. But sometimes this perfect symmetry is achieved by the strangest, irregular, odd-angled means.

No paintings have survived to tell us whether the Ancient Greeks knew about perspective in paintings—but they certainly exploited it in building temples. The greatest Greek temple, the Parthenon in Athens, appears from a distance to be perfectly rectangular, but its columns are actually

subtly distorted. The corner columns are actually set closer together than the central columns, being 6 feet (1.8 m) apart at the corners and 8 feet (2.4 m) at the center. The base of the long front itself curves gently upward at the center while the corner columns lean inward. The columns themselves are thicker half way up than they are the top. None of this is obvious from a distance, but it gives the Parthenon an appearance of perfect symmetry as it rises on the hill of the Acropolis above the city.

Such visual tricks with perspective returned with the Renaissance. The painter and architect Giotto (1267-1337) was commissioned to design the freestanding campanile (belltower) of Florence Cathedral in 1334. The space in which he had to build the tower was very cramped, so tall buildings often appear to lean backward when viewed from close up. To avoid this, Giotto built his tower so that it became gradually wider toward the top. From the ground, this divergence counteracts the effect of perspective and makes the tower look perfectly straight and upright. Like many Renaissance architects, Giotto had a mystical belief in perfectly proportioned buildings, which symbolized human and divine harmony.

STRAIGHT UP

The great campanile (belltower) of Florence Cathedral (*left*), built in the 1300s, appears quite perpendicular, but in fact, it swells out gently toward the top. This makes it look straight to observers on the ground.

DID YOU KNOW?
The strange palazzo

MOST RENAISSANCE ARTISTS had an almost religious belief in symmetry. But one Italian architect had rather different ideas. Francesco Borromini (1599-1667), one of the greatest architects of the 1600s, had a taste for the unexpected.

In the Palazzo Spada in Rome, built for a Cardinal Spada in 1652, he designed a colonnade (*above, below and right*) which

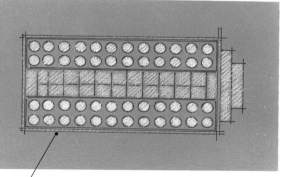

plan view

elevation

almost seems to laugh at Renaissance obsessions with perfect perspective. In the palace is a small colonnaded corridor just 40 feet (12 m) long. But Borromini has made it look far longer by making the two sides converge and reducing the height of the columns as they recede. A bizarre side effect of this weird perspective is that people seem to grow as they walk away down the corridor. Few modern architects have designed anything so amusingly illusionistic.

IN CAMERA

The very same rules of linear perspective the Renaissance artists used to paint realistic scenes can be seen in action in camera images. Although the first practical photographic process was invented by Louis Daguerre in 1837, the basic idea of the camera was known in Ancient China thousands of years ago.

In the fifth century B.C., a Chinese philosopher named Mo Ti noticed that light shining through a pinhole in a silk screen into a darkened room projected a vague, upsidedown picture of the world outside on to the opposite wall. But the first to put this observation to practical use were the Arabian astronomers of the eleventh century. Since it was dangerous to look at the sun directly, the Arabian astronomers studied eclipses by projecting them through a tiny hole on to the wall of a darkened room. Later, a room like this came to be called a *camera obscura* which is Latin for "darkened room".

In the Renaissance, a young Italian scientist, Giovanni Porta, described in his book *Natural Magic* how a lens could be placed in the pinhole to give a much sharper image. The camera obscura soon became popular with all kinds of people, especially artists, who used them to trace an accurate outline of their subject. It was soon realized that the camera did not have to be the size of a room; it could simply be a portable box with a viewing screen at the back. By the 1600s, many artists were using portable models about 2 feet (60 cm) across with a double convex glass lens, which enhanced its power.

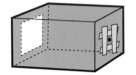

BASIC CAMERA

A paperboard box (*above*), with a tracing paper screen at one end, and a 1inch (25 mm) hole in the other. Tape tinfoil over this hole, and pierce it in the center. Take the box to a window, cover yourself and the box (*right*), leaving the foil end open, and look through the window. An upsidedown image of the scene in front appears on the tracing paper.

UPDATE

The modern camera (*right*) is simply a sophisticated version of the camera obscura.

Corrected image

Lens

Inverted image

Mirror reverses upside down image.

3-D INTERIOR

Samuel van Hoogstraten's
peepshow (*above*) is the most
famous camera obscura to
survive intact. Inside, he
painted a Dutch interior which,
when viewed through the
peephole, looks lifesize—see
just how it works on the
following page.

The photographic process invented by Daguerre and in cameras ever
since simply uses light-sensitive chemicals to record the image projected inside such a box.

PEEP SHOW

A variant of the camera obscura is the peepshow, first designed by
Alberti in the 1400s to demonstrate perspective. The peepshow
consists of a box with scenes painted on the inside which are
illuminated by a light source (daylight or lamp) on one side. With only
a single possible viewpoint, it gives viewers a powerful illusion of
three-dimensional reality.

To the viewer looking through the peephole at the scene below, it seems as if he is looking through a window, where a shaft of light falls on the checked floor.

The most ingenious peepshow was constructed by the Dutch artist Samuel van Hoogstraten (1627-78), a pupil of Rembrandt and a writer on art. Hoogstraten was influenced by Alberti and other Renaissance writers but he carried their obsession with perspective farther. He was fascinated by trompe l'oeil effects (see pp. 24-5) and the distortions of

anamorphosis (*see Chapter 3*). In his most ambitious work, Hoogstraten combined the two concepts. The inside is exquisitely painted with a representation of a simple, but well-lit Dutch interior which looks life-sized when viewed through the peephole. On the lid of the box, he painted an ingenious picture of Venus and Cupid in bed stretched out so that it can only be seen correctly by looking over the box from the right. In the painting itself, the walls, windows and even the dog appear distorted. But seen correctly through the peepholes, they appear remarkably realistic. You seem to be looking into a three-dimensional room, like a Vermeer interior come to life.

HOW IT WORKS: Hoogstraten's hall

UNLIKE MOST PEEPSHOWS, Hoogstraten's box had two peepholes. They are actually exactly opposite each other, but they appear to be slightly offset.

Left hand view of room

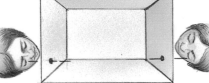

Plan view of peepshow

Dog as actually painted

Right hand view of room

By tracing lines of sight on the diagram from the peephole P to the corners of the projected room A, B, and C, you can work out how Hoogstraten constructed his image. The line PA intersects the box at X, which is where the lid and front wall of the box (close to the aperture) join. The line PB intersects the lid at Y and the line PC cuts the back wall at Z. The top of the projected wall AB had be painted along real XY, and the imaginary wall AC painted along XZ. The end wall of the room had to be painted on three planes to be convincing.

The real base of the wall MN seems to be in a straight line with ZM, but is actually continued by the projected MC. Although it sounds complex, it is actually a fine example of single viewpoint perspective with all the orthogonal lines (see p.12) converging to the vanishing point when viewed, as intended, from the peephole.

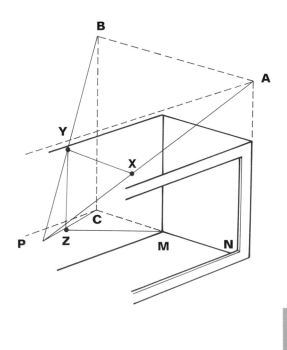

TROMPE L'OEIL: tricking the eye

By exploiting perspective, shadows and texture, artists and architects can create remarkable illusions called trompe l'oeil— literally, "trick the eye". Sometimes these can be so convincing that you can hardly tell what is real and what is painted even when you know it is an illusion.

The trompe-l'oeil effect (*below*), part of a mural in an Italian restaurant, gives diners the impression they are looking heavenwards.

"Father" Andrea Pozzo
ENTRY OF ST IGNATIUS INTO HEAVEN
The saint soars into highest heaven (*above*) past architecture which seems solid, but is, in fact, a magnificent feat of trompe l'oeil art.

One of the first artists to use the trompe l'oeil effect was Giotto. As a young apprentice, he is said to have painted a fly on the nose of a figure which was so lifelike that his master Cimabue tried to brush it off several times before realizing it was painted. But the Renaissance masterpiece of **trompe l'oeil** is the ceiling in the ducal palace of Mantua, northern Italy, painted by Andrea Mantegna (1431-1506). This ceiling is painted in such a way that the whole room seems much, much higher than it really is—an effect called *quadratura*.

The greatest exponent of trompe l'oeil painting was the Baroque artist Andrea Pozzo (1642-1709). Because he became a lay brother in the Jesuit Order, he is sometimes given the courtesy title Father Pozzo, but he was not a priest, and simply worked for the Jesuits as a painter and architect. His masterpiece is the huge fresco he made for the ceiling of the nave of the church of S. Ignazio in Rome 1691-94. Here the blue and gold heavens seem to open as Saint Ignazio ascends jubilantly towards Jesus. Not only is Pozzo's sky remarkably convincing; it is hard to tell where the actual architecture ends and the painted architecture around its base begins.

Pozzo was a great influence on later trompe l'oeil painters, among them the Venetian painter Giambattista Tiepolo (1697-1770) whose masterpiece of trompe l'oeil is the Grand Staircase of the bishop's palace at Würzburg, Germany.

Among the great modern masters of trompe l'oeil was the Surrealist painter René Magritte (1898-1967), whose enigmatic pictures give the everyday world a strange, dreamlike quality. Pictured below is *Euclidean Walks* (1955), a perfectly proportioned perspective view, which is transformed into a mystery by the canvas on the easel in front of the window which itself shows the identical view. It is very hard to tell where the picture within the picture ends and the outer picture starts. There is a further playful piece of trompe l'oeil in the way the conical tower on the canvas within the picture closely resembles the perspective of the receding street. Magritte loved painting such visual puns, but they all work only because his viewers, brought up in the Western tradition, automatically accept his perspectives.

Among the most remarkably realistic trompe l'oeil artists today is Sarah Janson, whose *Architectural Trompe l'Oeil* on board the cruise ship "Oriana", utterly convinces onlookers they are gazing at a real life silver collection in a cabinet, with its deep shadows and gleaming metal.

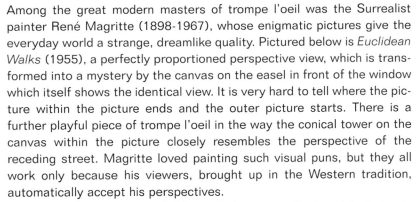

René Magritte

EUCLIDEAN WALKS

A picture within a picture as Magritte teases the viewer with the easel before the window, and with the tower's conical roof transformed into a convincing street.

DID YOU KNOW?
Hogarth's lesson

WILLIAM HOGARTH (1697-1764) was the first great British painter, renowned for his satirical engravings such as *The Rake's Progress*. But he also wanted to found a national British school of painting. To illustrate how not to draw perspective—and there were many incompetent painters around—he produced the engraving *False Perspective* in 1754. This had the caption: "Whoever makes a Design without the knowledge of Perspective will be liable to such Absurdities as are shown on this frontispiece."

At first sight, Hogarth's engraving is an idyllic landscape, but really it is a masterpiece of false perspective. The fisherman in the foreground drops his line beyond that of the fisherman in the middle distance, while the inn sign is supported by posts running into both the shed and the house beyond it—clearly impossible. Illusory too is the woman in the inn window giving a light to the distant smoker on the horizon, while the perspective of the river has gone drastically wrong.

THEATRICAL ILLUSIONS

Illusion has always played a central role in the dramatic art, from the days of the Ancient Greeks to the musical spectaculars of today, and theaters have long exploited perspective painting to deceive the eye.

One of the oldest theatrical sets is the *Teatro Olympico* (Olympian Theater) at Vicenza, Italy. Designed by the Renaissance architect Andrea Palladio (1508-80), it was a reconstruction of an ancient Roman theater, with a semicircular auditorium and permanent scenery. Behind the solid architectural façade on stage, four gateways reveal vistas lined with palaces and temples, stretching away in perfect perspective, giving the impression of a great city. In fact, all are made only of wooden fronts which recede according to the Renaissance theories of Sebastiano Serlio, who had described theatrical perspective in his book *Architettura* (1545).

The problem with fixed scenery like this was that it was suitable only for city scenes. Then, in the 1600s, the English architect and stage designer Inigo Jones, who first introduced proper Renaissance architecture to the English-speaking world, invented a way of introducing movable scenery. Until this time, performances in English theater—like the first performances of Shakespeare's plays at the Globe and similar theatres in London—had been played on a bare, open stage with virtually no scenery. Inigo Jones's idea was to frame the stage with a proscenium arch so that it seemed like the view through a window. For plays like *Florimène*, performed in 1635, he tried to make the audience —at least in the center of the theater—feel that it was really looking through the window at a peaceful wooded scene. On the

TEATRO OLYMPICO
Palladio's stage scenery (*below*) provided one compelling illusion of a city receding behind the gateways but only one illusion, as it was a fixed stage.

stage, Jones set up movable "flats"—rectangular canvas screens painted with scenery and then carefully aligned on a single vanishing point deep within the stage. The flats would be arranged in a series leading the eye back along the wings of the stage, which is why they were sometimes called wings.

Obviously, it was vital that the painters of each flat or wing worked according to a carefully conceived overall design—which itself required a full understanding of the practise of perspective. Part of the perspective behind the proscenium was real depth and part-painted screens, and the two needed careful balancing.

Another innovation, which is still in use, was raking, or inclining, the stage so slightly as to be imperceptible. This helped members of the audience in the back seats see farther onto the stage and also increased the illusion of depth. This trick is still widely used today, although some designers now wildly exaggerate the rake of the stage.

In 1771 Philippe de Loutherbourg, a French artist who had worked in Italy, began working for the actor/manager David Garrick at Drury Lane, then London's leading theater. De Loutherbourg epitomized the new romantic spirit of the age with his melodramatic scenery, often with wild forest or mountain backcloths. His approach was that of a painter, not an architect, and he tried to suggest infinite misty panoramas rather than ordered city streets. He partly broke with traditional perspective by using raked wings and flats set at various angles and much of his impact came from using lighting dramatically.

STAGE SET

The architect Inigo Jones pioneered painted stage scenery in Britain with the poetic, yet mathematically exact perspective of the scenery painted on flats for the play *Florimène* (*above*).

CHAPTER 2

OPTICAL CONFUSIONS

Every moment your eyes are open, your mind is trying to interpret what you see—deciding whether this square of lines is a book, or that circle is a plate. You cannot look at the world without your mind imposing its interpretation. Fortunately, its analysis is remarkably accurate most of the time. Indeed it has to be, for you could not survive if you were unable to tell the difference between a car wheel and a plate of chips. Yet the very insistence of your mind's analsyis of what the eye sees can lead it into illusion. Hungarian-born painter Victor Vasarely has tried to create a hallucinatory impression of movement through paintings that are visually ambigous, as in Vonal Strie (1975, left). Do you see it as it is, simply squares of colored lines? Or does your mind insist on showing you something else?

FIRST IMPRESSIONS

All through our lives, the brain works with the eye to make sense of the world. Early in childhood, it begins to decipher the images registered in the eye, learning to instantly recognize important shapes from the slightest clues. We know that a coin is round, or a window or doorway rectangular even when we see them only glancingly at an angle. But this very cleverness in recognition means that the eye and brain can sometimes be fooled by misleading clues.

Humans rely overwhelmingly on eyesight to deal with the world. We tend to remember, recall, identify, and even dream mainly in images. "I never forget a face," some say, when forgetting the name and everything else about a person. We are visually attuned creatures. But when familiar objects are surrounded or crossed by totally unexpected and unusual patterns which simply do not occur in nature, the eye-brain partnership can be thrown into confusion, like a computer wrongly programmed.

It is known that these confusions occur, but it is not yet clear to scientists exactly how they happen. Significantly, people who have suffered strokes which affect a certain part of the brain may have difficulty in recognizing a familiar object, such as a bucket seen from an unfamiliar angle. It is our minds which finally decide, and their decisions are undoubtedly preconditioned, as reactions to the picture at the top of the next page demonstrate.

People brought up in the Western tradition will tend to "read" or interpret this drawing as a house interior. They see a family sitting inside their room with a corner in the center background and a window just above the head of the young woman seated on the left, with a plant of some sort visible through it. This is partly due to the hint of depth which the corner of the room provides and partly because westerners expect to see a family sitting inside a living-room. People from rural Africa, by

DID YOU KNOW?
Gothic arches

IF YOU WANDER AROUND inside a Gothic church or cathedral with tall arches separating off side aisles and chapels, you may notice a strange phenomenon. From certain points, the front arches overlap the farther rows so that the points of the arches no longer appear to close symmetrically at their apex. Instead, they seem to meet off-center in a rather irregular fashion. This is not actually the case, for Gothic architecture is generally regular. What is happening is that the overlapping contours of the arches have confused the eye, as the diagram shows.

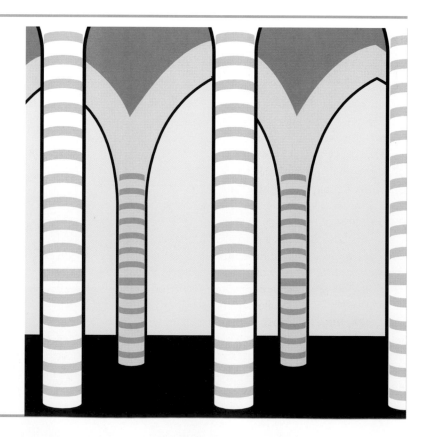

A QUESTION OF UPBRINGING
Your perception of the family scene (*above*) will differ according to your experience of life. A rural African would place the family outside; a northern European would see the inside of a room.

Which line is longer (*below*)? Make a guess, and then measure them against a ruler to see what is known as the Müller-Lyer effect in action.

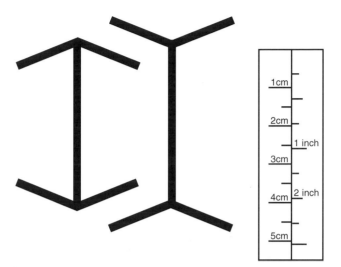

contrast, see a family seated outside, under the trunk of a tree (not a corner), with the young woman balancing a gasoline can on her head—a common sight in some rural areas. Not only do people see what they are used to seeing around them but also they fail to "read" clues they are unfamiliar with. We all tend to see what we expect.

THE MÜLLER-LYER EFFECT

One of the most common mistakes our brain's snap prejudgments leads us into is over relative size. The illustration (*above right*) shows two lines, called Müller-Lyer lines after the German physiologist Johannes Müller, who discovered them in 1840. The line with outward-pointing arrows seems to be much shorter than the other. In fact it is exactly the same length. You can measure this with a ruler. To make the "short" arrow look the same length as the other, it actually needs to be drawn deliberately longer.

Even more remarkably, the Müller-Lyer effect operates equally strongly in three-dimensional real life. No-one knows exactly why two horizontal or vertical lines persistently appear to be of different size, even after you have measured them and found they are quite identical in length; it is yet another example of the mystery of optical illusion.

Your eye can become similarly confused when what are in reality parallel diagonal lines are inter-sected by vertical lines. The small "herringbone" pattern cross-lines appear ragged and discont-inous. Once again, if you check with a ruler, you will find that they are all in reality perfectly continuous diagonals.

TEMPLE OF CONFUSION

Are the columns (*above*) absolutely perpendicular? Check them out with a ruler to find out just how the extra decorative effects can deceive your eye.

Horizontal lines also appear to bend or swell when the eye is confused by superimposed shapes. This confusion of parallels is what is called the Zöllner Illusion and, as can be seen from the fantastic temple illustration (*left*), can even extend to full-scale pictures. The temple columns appear to taper or expand. If you judge by your eyes alone, you would find it almost impossible to guess that they are all completely parallel, so great is the optical confusion caused by the slanting lines around them. But if you measure the columns with a ruler, you will again find that they are completely perpendicular and parallel.

A

B

REAL-LIFE CONFUSION

The photographs of the door (*above*) are identical. But depending on your focus the central column can look different lengths: longer in A than in B, although, of course they are the same.

FIRST IMPRESSIONS

33

HORIZONTALS AND VERTICALS

People have used vertical and horizontal lines and stripes for centuries to decorate buildings, clothes, and even their bodies. But lines like these are not always just decorative; sometimes they affect the way your eyes perceive objects, making them appear smaller or larger.

Sometimes, even the simplest of intrusions into a shape can baffle the eye. The two striped rectangles (*below left*) appear different. The horizontally striped shape on the right appears taller; the vertically striped shape on the left appears wider. In fact both are identical squares. In general, horizontal stripes make an area look higher while vertical stripes make it appear wider. This can be seen from the piles of coins (*below*). The stack on the right seems as high as it is broad. In fact, the stack on the left is equally wide and high, but the circular stripes around the coins fool the eye. Medieval architects knew about and exploited this effect. They gave the columns of cathedrals such as that in Siena, Italy horizontal stripes partly to make them appear taller. Oddly, the effect is not always apparent on people, for vertically striped clothes tend to make the wearer appear look taller and thinner, while broad, horizontal stripes will emphasize breadth.

SQUARE DEAL

WHICH OF THESE is as wide as it is tall?

BULGY SQUARES

Few shapes appear more unmistakably regular and stable than a square. But squares too can bulge and quiver as though they were made of jelly when strongly incongruous patterns are superimposed on them. In the examples above, the first and fourth squares, one surrounded by circles, the other by squares, seem to bend inward. The second example, surrounded by concave lines, seems to bulge outward. The square filled with diagonal lines arrowing down, seems to become almost trapezoid and appear wider at the bottom than at the top. All these are illusions, for the squares are perfectly square.

SQUASHING SQUARES

You can experiment with bulging or squashed squares yourself, by taking or drawing the figure of a basic, unadorned square on a sheet of paper, then adding different types of lines around it. You will be amazed to notice how the shapes appear to distort.

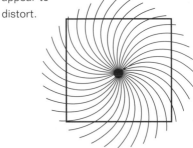

PONZO LINES

One of the most compelling examples of optical confusion is the Ponzo distortion. This consists of three horizontal bars of identical length placed one above the other inside two lines converging on a distant vanishing point, such as railroad lines in a photograph, or simply converging lines. When perspective is depicted on a flat plane, the upper bar is interpreted—at least by anyone accustomed to linear perspective—as being larger than the next band below and so on.

Interestingly, people brought up outside the Western tradition of linear perspective—for example, Africans, who have grown up in round houses which lack right angles—appear less likely to be deceived by Ponzo lines than westerners.

SIGNS AND SYMBOLS

The world around us is full of signs and symbols. Many of these rely on the same processes that create optical illusions—the willingness of the brain to interpret what the eye sees.

WORDLESS WARNINGS

A warning is useless if it is not understood by those it is intended for. So many warning signs are wordless to overcome language barriers. They convey the message in a kind of visual shorthand readily understandable to anyone who sees them. Some are obvious, like the curved line to warn of a bend in the road, or the silhouette of an aircraft to indicate an airport. Some are part of a visual language so familiar that we no longer think about it as being a language. A diagonal line indicates something is forbidden. A red sign indicates danger.

The image of a deer (*above*) speaks more directly than words.

Evocative pictorial warning of falling rocks (*above*).

Signs (*below*) to be read while stationary, and designed for speed reading (*right*).

Emergency vehicles (*below*), often have their lettering reversed to be read the right way in drivers' rearview

SPEED READING

Many signs have to be read from fast-moving vehicles. To make this easier, some signs are distorted anamorphically. If they were not distorted, they would only be seen as a blur. Similarly, signs on the fronts of ambulances are both reversed and distorted anamorphically so that drivers, glancing in their rearview mirrors can recognize the word instantly.

SYMBOLS OF POWER

Some signs have acquired such potency by their associations that they invoke a strong reaction—even though they are simply lines on paper or simple shapes. The simple vertical and horizontal lines of the Christian cross are loaded with religious and emotional meaning for any Christian, just as the curves of the Islamic crescent are for Moslems. The swastika, once the Hindu symbol for good luck, now has the power to evoke shock, fear and outrage because of its association with the Nazis.

The reversed swastiki (*above*) is the Hindu symbol for good luck—seen here on this Indian stall selling pulses and spices.

The swastika (*right*) has become associated with the sinister power of the Nazis. Yet it is only a simple geometric symbol.

Deutschland, deine kolonien!

AMBIGUOUS IMAGES

With your eyes and brain you constantly make judgments about the world in front of you—"is it a bird?...is it a plane?...or could it be both?" Some things leave your eyes and brain bewildered, for they have two (at least) possible interpretations. They are ambiguous images.

The eye and brain are very quick to judge, making decisions about what we see almost instantly—and once they have made their snap decision, it is very difficult to see things otherwise. When looking at a picture of a person in a scene, for instance, we make a strong and instant distinction between the figure and the background scene. If we did not, the picture would become meaningless blotches of tone or color. But there is a potential for ambiguity in even the simplest line drawing in pencil or ink and such snap decisions may turn out to be wrong.

DOUBLE MEANINGS

The brain makes such strong decisions about an object's identity that it can be disconcerting when it is shown to be wrong. A picture which seems to show the outline of a tree in full leaf can be changed into the profile of a woman smoking by the addition of just a tiny cigarette-like shape. What makes such images disturbing is that identification shifts continually from one subject to another as you look at them.

It has long been recognized that not just the eye but the mind is involved in such misreadings of ambiguous images. In the past, psychologists used Rorschach ink spots (*left and below*) to try to gauge personality. The Swiss psychiatrist, Hermann Rorschach, who introduced the test, used ten basic blots, five in black and white, five in color, and asked the subject to interpret them. Of course, almost anything can be read into such irregular, unformed shapes. This technique probably has limited value as a diagnostic tool for reflecting someone's state of mind. But the multiplicity of interpretations indicates the powerful role the mind plays in shaping what we see.

One factor all ambiguous pictures have in common is that when they change, they do so dramatically. As you make a new identification, every feature alters its meaning or significance so sharply that you may find it hard to believe that the picture itself has not been changed by a hidden trick. You may even be fooled into thinking you must have subtly changed your viewpoint to produce the change. But the shifts happen only in the mind.

INK SPOT PSYCHOLOGY
What do you see in the inkspots (*above and below left*)—a demon, an animal, a garland? Your interpretation could give a clue to your personality to a clinical psychologist. Knives are said to show hostility...perceiving movement suggests imagination.

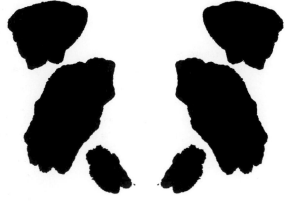

FOREGROUND AND BACKGROUND

Glance at a simple drawing like the one on the right and you may see the white silhouette of a vase against a blue background. But if you blink or look away for a moment, the image may suddenly become a pair of faces in profile facing each other against a white background.

Edgar Rubin, the Danish psychologist who devised these images, made the important observation that what the brain tries to do is make a distinction between a shape in the foreground and a shapeless background. Rubin described this process as "reading" an image, for we "read" the external world in a way roughly similar to reading a book, making an instant distinction between the meaningful letters and the meaningless page. Understanding the real world requires us to interpret just as we must interpret letters to understand writing.

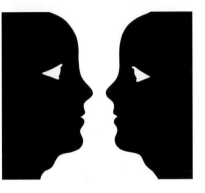

WHAT CAN YOU SEE?

Do you see black tools or cream? Whichever you see, you can discover the total number of both on pp.122-3.

DEFINING SHAPES

If visual clues are added to the ambiguous images on this page, they become unambiguously either a vase or two faces. If you want to see a vase, add a bouquet of flowers. If you would prefer to look at two profiles facing each other, add a couple of appropriately placed eyes. It is remarkable how such small touches so clearly define the image either way to the observer.

PRECONCEPTIONS DISTURBED

Ambiguous images are often encountered in the world. Many a child has been frightened by the strange shadow in the dark that looked like a monster. As psychologists have become interested in the way the mind perceives the world, so artists have deliberately devised ambiguous images both for research and for fun.

WHAT DO YOU SEE?
A duck...or, blink again...a rabbit? It depends on whether you view from left or right.

Typical of such ambiguous images is the duck/rabbit. If you look at it from the right, you can see the duck's open beak and its bright eye, seen in profile above its long neck. But if you blink and look at the image from the left you have a rabbit with its eye looking leftwards and its long ears standing out behind it. And while you are looking at the duck it may eerily metamorphose into a rabbit—or vice-versa!

One of the most famous ambiguous images is the cartoon of *My Mother-in-Law/My Wife* devised by W. E. Hill in 1915. At first sight, it appears to be a sketch of a beautiful young woman, looking over her right shoulder so that only the tip of her nose and left eyelash are visible beneath her dark hair and the charming white feather. A scarf on top sets off her face as do a fur wrap and black band around her neck beneath. Yet if you look again you may see an embittered old woman, with a huge gaunt nose taking the place of the young beauty's delicate chin and cheek, a sharp jaw jutting out, and eyes sunk deep in her face. There is something almost Freudian in the unease which this sudden transformation from youthful beauty to withered age can produce.

You can see a similar sudden process of rapid aging in the companion picture drawn a few years later by Jack Botwinick, *Husband/Father-in-Law*. The keen, young man with his hat shading the left of his face, turns in an instant into an old sailor with his sunken chin and lopsided hat. Both are grim reminders of growing old.

W. E. Hill
MY MOTHER-IN-LAW/MY WIFE
The way this image (*above*) reverses itself from a beautiful young girl to a wizened and miserable-looking old woman is highly disconcerting. It is often called, rather misogynistically, My Wife/My Mother-in-Law.

Jack Botwinick
HUSBAND/FATHER-IN-LAW
Turn the page upsidedown to see a subtle example of a reversible image (*left*), and another reminder of galloping senescence.

Gustave Verbeek
UPSIDEDOWN
You need to invert Gustave Verbeek's cartoon (*above*) to see its other meaning.

NATIVE AMERICANS
Look at the image (below *right*) with the left hand shape as the foreground figure and the rest as the background, you will see an Inuit in fur-lined coat stretching out his right hand into the shadow. But if you start by taking the right hand shadow as the figure, the figure emerges of a native American Indian in profile, with thick black hair and chiseled features.

Far more cheerful are the *Upsidedown* series of cartoons drawn by Gustave Verbeek, which appeared in *The New York Herald* as a comic strip from 1903 to 1905. The best, illustrated above, shows one of Verbeek's favorite characters, Lady Lovekins being picked up by a Roc, a giant mythical bird which is standing on an island. But turn the picture upsidedown to see an island, trees, and a mischievous fish waving its tail alarmingly at another character—old Mufarroo's—in his canoe.

Such ambiguity can be incorporated even into lettering. In the type of lettering known as Shadow Antiqua ("Granby shadow"), you can see what seem to be the shadows cast on the right of the side of the letters by a light source. This gives them a three-dimensional appearance—as though they were casting shadows.

PRECONCEPTIONS DISTURBED

41

AMBIGUOUS ART

Artists have always enjoyed playing with their power to create illusions. By creating deliberately ambivalent images, they can tantalize you. Nothing in art is as it seems.

Artists have been exploiting eye-teasing ambiguities for thousands of years. In the days of the Roman Empire, the craftsmen who made mosaic floors for the wealthy citizens capitalized on the human eye's ability to switch between different readings. In a Roman mosaic floor in Antioch, Turkey, you can read the cubes in the pattern either as solid cubes lit from above or as hollow cubes lit from below. Similarly, when you look at the swirling mosaic from a floor such as those popular in ancient Rome, your eye will search for the point on which to center the whole spiral—in vain. There is no such point and you can never determine firmly which of the overlapping arcs is supposed to be above the other.

DID YOU KNOW?
Mussolini's head

AMBIGUITY is most easily contrived in pictures, but occasionally it can be set up in three-dimensional objects. One of the best examples is by the Italian artist Renato Bertelli (1900-1974), now lodged in the Imperial War Museum, London. Bertelli carved a black marble newel post (the central pillar of a winding stair). When viewed by an observer, this can disconcertingly transform itself into the profile of the Italian dictator Benito Mussolini—a transformation helped by the way Mussolini used to shave his bullet-like head.

ESCHER'S TRICKS

No artist has explored the ambiguous more thoroughly than Dutch artist Maurits Cornelis Escher (1898-1972). In his haunting series of lithographic prints, he captures the secrets and ambiguities of perspective and optical illusions in a remarkable way.

Escher's art tends to appeal especially to those of a mathematical bent, for although in many ways similar to some Surrealist pictures, his art is in fact severely intellectual. In earlier works, such as *Eight Heads*, Escher was merely playing with the possibilities of ambiguity, and the results are quite simple. Here the repeated pattern of heads turns into a frieze of quite different heads when inverted. But when he came to design a famous lithograph such as *Concave and Convex*, he confessed: "I spent more than a whole month brooding over this picture, because my initial drafts were all far too complicated to make head or tail of."

Concave and Convex is nightmarishly ambiguous. It appears at first sight symmetrical, the building being composed of two halves, one the near-mirror image of the other, dividing in the middle. But, if you try to follow any of the human figures climbing up and down the numerous stairs, you find that, as you cross the center, everything turns inside out and the convex becomes concave (or vice-versa) as you look at it.

A woman on the top left of the picture carrying a basket is about to descend a flight of stairs onto a landing where there is a small basin. But that basin is also the shell decoration of a ceiling to which two lizards are glued and she is in danger of falling into the void! The

staircase on the right turns into a stepped vault supporting an arch. The entire picture is full of such reversals of convexity and concavity, which tease the mind's eye. The more you look, the more confusing is the image: as the artist himself commented, " In my opinion, an impossible situation only really stands out when the impossibility is not immediately obvious...There should be a certain mysteriousness that does not immediately hit the eye."

M. C. Escher
CIRCLE LIMIT
Angels and devils alternate (*above*) and switch between foreground and background.

43

THE SURREALISTS

Earlier this century, Surrealist artists such as René Magritte and Salvador Dali began to explore the limits and oddities of the human unconsciousness in their own unique way. The result was a series of bizarre ambiguous paintings.

Salvador Dali

THE METAMORPHOSIS OF NARCISSUS, 1933

Dali's reworking of the Greek myth *(below)* is dreamlike, both in its psychological power and in its ambiguity.

The Surrealist movement used ambiguity in their paintings to explore and expose the "more real behind the real." Influenced by the work of Sigmund Freud in psychoanalysis, they plumbed the inner depths of the human mind—the interior worlds of fantasy, memory, and dreams for inspiration. Salvador Dalì (1940-1989), in particular, delighted in baffling observers with ambiguous imagery. In his painting *The Metamorphosis of Narcissus (below)*, the central figure switches as you look at it, from being a crouching human figure to a gigantic hand holding an egg. In *Swans Reflecting Elephants*, Dalì perfected this dreamlike ambiguity. The graceful, long-necked swans floating on the water change into heavy-legged elephants in what is literally a mirror image.

Belgian painter René Magritte (1898-1967) was fascinated by Kafkaesque ambiguity. His painting *Gigantic Days* is a particularly disturbing work. It could either be a woman being assaulted by a man or

Sandro del Prete
THE WINDOW OPPOSITE
Is the woman (*below*) inside or outside?

a woman metamorphosing, clearly much against her will, into a man. Magritte painted more gentle ambiguous works such as *The Domain of Arnheim (above)* where an eagle embedded in a mountain ridge seems to have laid its eggs on the window ledge.

The contemporary artist Sandro del Prete plays with subconscious erotic preconceptions in *The Window Opposite (right)*. Here the eye switches between seeing a naked woman, hanging in improbable peril against a wall, and the same woman, safely inside a window, her lower body obscured by a wine glass and window ledge from which hang her stockings.

45

DOUBLE MEANINGS

You can make images very easily yourself by building pictures up with cut-outs. The secret is to look for corresponding shapes.

FISH IN TANK OR GIRL WITH FRINGE?

Flesh   *Yellow*   *Gold*

Blue   *White*   *Brown*

THIS DOUBLE PICTURE takes its cue from the correspondence in shape between a girl's eye and a fish. The stylized approach to the picture allows the fishes' eyes to be drawn bug-eyed as if they were the girl's pupils—but the need for them to be near the head of the fish has given the girl an intense, almost cross-eyed stare.

COLORS must be carefully chosen for these double-meanings to work. In the version on the left, we quite happily accept that weeds can be golden and water can be pale yellow. We even accept that fishes' eyes can be blue. But try coloring the picture below as a real fish scene with green reeds, blue water and brown eyes—and see what happens to the girl!

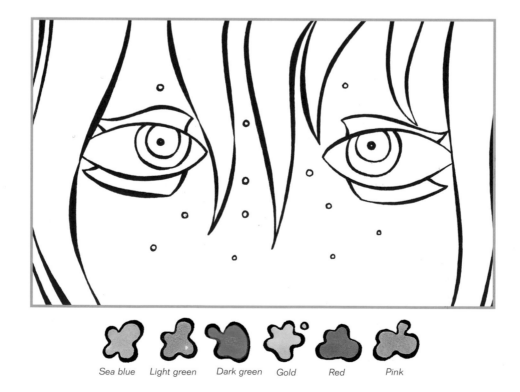

Sea blue   *Light green*   *Dark green*   *Gold*   *Red*   *Pink*

CHRISTMAS TREE OR BOAT?

Russet   *Green*   *Sea blue*

Purple   *White*   *Indigo*

CHOICE OF COLOR can transform the meaning of a picture. No yacht has green sails. No Christmas tree has white leaves. Or does it?

Blue   *Green*   *Red*   *Brown*   *Yellow*

OTHER IDEAS

ONE OF THE BEST WAYS to create double-meaning pictures is simply to play around with simple shapes. Try drawing a few strong, bold shapes on the page—and then work out just how many things they can be. Once you have an idea, refine it and color it.

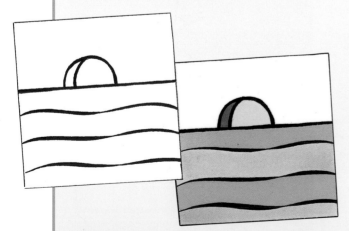

THE SIMPLER and bolder the shapes, the more meanings they may have. Is this sunrise? A floating beach ball? Or a jockey behind a screen?

THE MEANING OF SOME IMAGES is transformed simply by turning them the other way up. Here a rotund, mad, yellow-eyed character is also a tired, glum pig.

47

THE SCIENTIFIC APPROACH

Scientists take an interest in tricks of the eye as well as artists—only they describe them as "optical ambiguity in depth and dimensions". One of the earliest scientific demonstrations of optical ambiguity is the Necker Cube.

Professor L. A. Necker was a Swiss mineralogist who drew a skeleton cube (of bare lines only) in 1832. His cube is drawn with parallel faces, without the convergence of normal perspective. What is remarkable is that, as you look at it, the cube suddenly reverses and what has been the leading face becomes the back face and vice-versa.

Necker puzzled over this strange phenomenon and in 1832 wrote to an English friend, Sir David Brewster: "We are dealing with a perceptual phenomenon in the field of optics...which I have observed many times when studying pictures of crystalline shapes."

He had noticed "a sudden involuntary change" in the apparent position of a crystal or similar three-dimensional body when it was reproduced on a two-dimensional surface.

"For a long time," Necker wrote, "I remained uncertain as to the explanation of this random and involuntary change...the only thing I was able to detect was an unusual sensation in the eye at the moment of change. To me this indicated an optical effect and not just (as I had at first thought) a mental one."

Necker was thus among the first to recognize that both eye and brain are involved in the interpretation of images. His discovery laid the groundwork for the scientific study of human perception in the twentieth century.

HOW IT WORKS: where's the star?

As YOU LOOK at the skeletal cube (*left and below*) the star's position changes in front of your eyes seemingly of its own uncanny volition. Is it at the front of the box, at the back or in the middle?

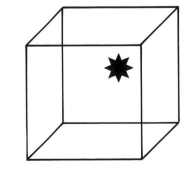 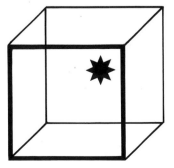 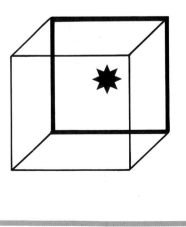

MACH'S FIGURE

One of the best examples of ambiguous images devised for scientific reasons is Ernst Mach's figure, the skeleton drawing of a half-open book. This could well be a book, your eye will tell you—but is the spine of the book thrust forward towards the observer? Or is the book open so that you are looking in to the spine, flanked by the open pages? It can be either, changing backwards and forwards in an eye-baffling instant.

WHAT CAN YOU SEE?

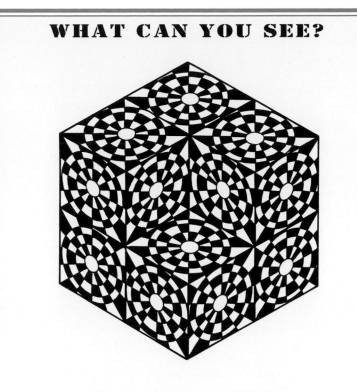

Do you see the front part of the cube coming forward towards you? Or is it going backwards, so the cube appears to be incomplete? It can be either, changing backwards and forwards before your very eyes!

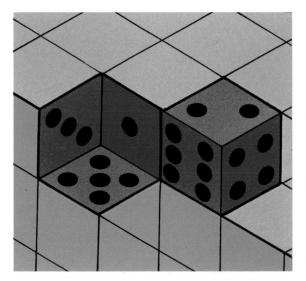

INSIDE OUT DICE

An elaboration of the basic principles of the Necker Cube, the pair of dice (*above*) turns concavity into convexity even as you look at them, the upside becoming the downside— which would make them hard to play with!

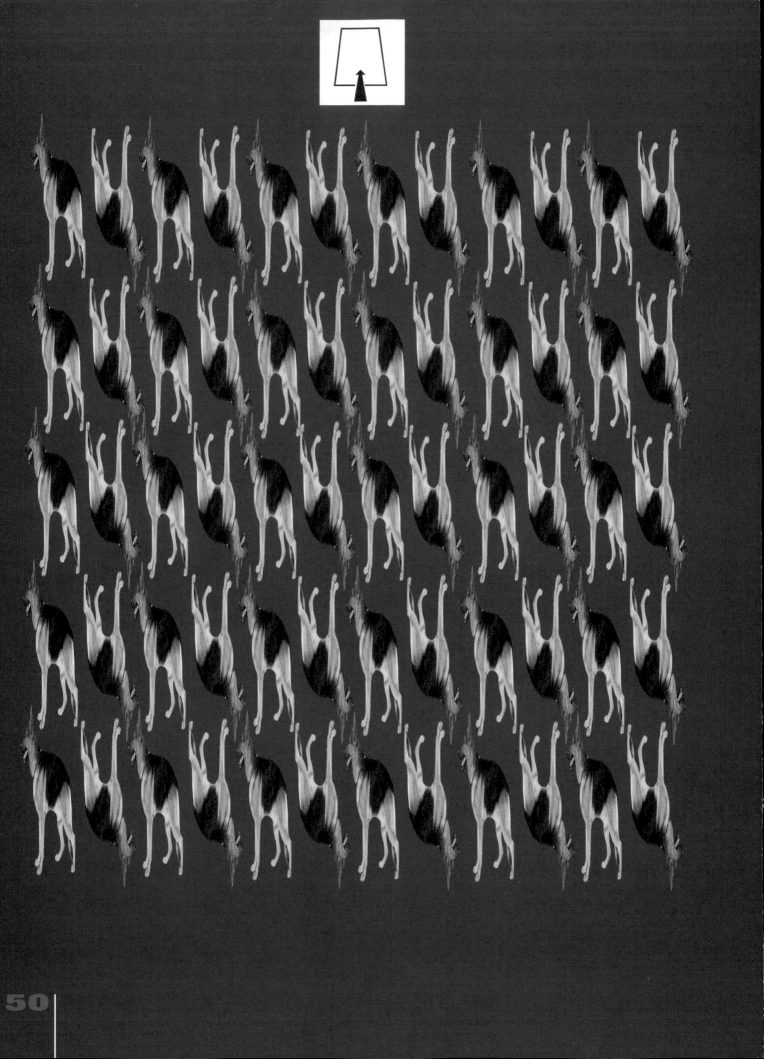

CHAPTER 3

ANAMORPHIC IMAGES

All the images on this double page look weird and stretched out if looked at from a normal point-of-view—as if a steamroller had been let loose in a pet sanctuary. Yet if you hold the edge of the book up flat to your eye and look across the page in the direction shown by the inset arrows, they begin to look like real cats and dogs. The pictures have not changed shape, of course, but our perception of the right perspective from this extreme angle transforms the distorted image into something more realistic. This kind of distortion is called anamorphic, and has attracted such great artists as Hans Holbein and Hoogstraten, who have used it to create mysterious illusions.

ARTISTIC DISTORTIONS

By the High Renaissance (1500-1520) most artists had mastered every technical aspect of perspective. Some began to develop tricks of perspective, the most remarkable of which was "anamorphosis"—the ancient Greek word for a transformed or distorted shape.

Anamorphosis has come to mean a way of painting a picture so that it only looks right when viewed from a peculiar angle, in a mirror or through a lens. Viewed normally, it appears so distorted that it may be virtually unrecognizable.

Perhaps the first great artist to explore the possibilities of anamorphosis was Leonardo da Vinci (1452-1519). Leonardo da Vinci was fascinated by every aspect of life and art and it seems only natural that he should explore the possibilities of perspective to their limits. There are many references to anamorphosis in his notebooks, but only one of his anamorphic works, a simple sketch in the collection of drawings known as the *Codex Atlanticus,* has survived.

STRETCHED IMAGE

If you hold your eye almost against the paper just beyond the left edge and squint, you can see the eight lines (above right) turn into a child's face.

HOLBEIN'S SKULL

The greatest work of anamorphic art was painted by Hans Holbein (1497-1543). A German artist originally from Augsburg, Holbein settled in England in 1532 to escape the religious turmoil of the Reformation in his homeland. In England, he painted realistic and yet psychologically revealing portraits of the rich and powerful.

Holbein was not altogether happy in England, and when in 1533 he came to paint his most celebrated painting, *The Ambassadors* (*right*), he added a morbid, enigmatic touch. The portrait, one of the largest ever painted, shows the French ambassador Jean de Dintville (*left*) and his friend Bishop Georges de Selve, portrayed full length and lifesize (which was unusual at the time). Dressed with aristocratic splendor, the two young Frenchmen are surrounded by books, and musical and scientific instruments which proclaim that they are men of learning in the Renaissance manner. Behind them the rich fabric of a green curtain adds a fitting touch of opulence. But when you actually look at the painting you cannot help noticing the strange, almost ghostly shape stretching diagonally across its foreground. It is in fact a human skull, but so distorted by anamorphosis as to be scarcely recognizable when viewed normally from the front. Holbein has added it to the portrait, as a *memento mori*—a reminder of death. Such grisly reminders were not uncommon in an age when life was very uncertain. To see the skull properly you need to stand at the bottom left corner of the picture and look up at it. Only then does the skull assume its proper alarming shape to give the whole portrait a very unusual feel.

HOW IT WORKS:
the anamorphic trick

IN THE 1500s, artists fascinated by perspective used to work out complex designs for anamorphosis on squared off tracing paper. They calculated precisely how different distortions would look to observers.

To see how anamorphosis works in Holbein's *The Ambassadors* (*above*), you would need to hang the picture on the wall of a staircase and then walk up and past it, keeping your eyes fixed on the skull the whole time. The effect can be shown in a computer simulation (*right*). As you approach the picture's left hand corner, the skull swims into proper perspective and then, as you continue, slides out again.

Hans Holbein

THE AMBASSADORS

Look at the elongated shape in the foreground, which makes this painting one of the best known works of anamorphic art.

DISTORTED KINGS

Soon after Holbein's *The Ambassadors* came another classic of anamorphosis. Dating from 1546, this is a much smaller picture—a portrait of the young prince who reigned briefly as King Edward VI from 1547 to 1553. The painting was once attributed to the Dutch painter William Scrotes who worked in England, but there is now some doubt over the real identity of the artist. Whoever painted it was clearly influenced by Holbein's experiment with anamorphism. Edward VI presents a weird appearance if seen from the front, with the prince's nose stretching out like Pinocchio's amid an elongated oval. But if you look at the picture from close to its right-hand side, the distortion vanishes and you see the prince as he really was: a rather anxious, sickly little boy.

An unexpected bonus of this sort of anamorphosis is that Prince Edward's head seems to protrude from the canvas in an almost three-dimensional way because of the way our eyes interpret the distorted shape. We find it difficult even to imagine the true shape of the distorted profile when viewed normally. So when we do realize its shape, we unconsciously read what we do see as a kind of three-dimensional phantom or ghost rising from the picture.

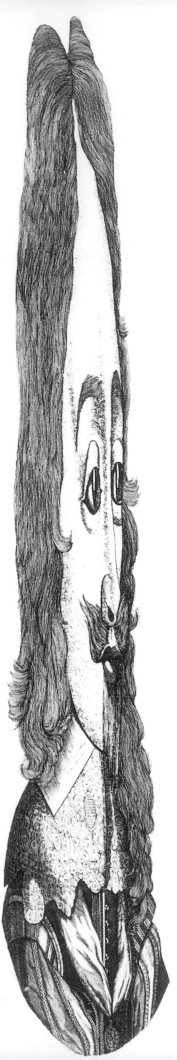

Ehard Schön

VEXIERBILD (PUZZLE PICTURE)

Schön was a Nuremberg engraver and a pupil of Dürer. This remarkable engraving, dating from around 1530, is one of a series Schön did, in which the slightly strange landscape of towns and hills, men and animals are created by striking anamorphic portraits. Look along this from the side, and you will see the river landscape becomes a young man interrupted in the midst of making love, throwing out an old man. The engraving is called, "Out, you old fool!"

PORTRAIT OF CHARLES I

After King Charles I's execution in 1649, anamorphic portraits of him like this (*right*) were distributed among royalists.

DID YOU KNOW?
The Shakespeare connection

IN 1598, fifty years after it was painted, Paul Hentzner, a German traveller in England saw the Prince Edward portrait displayed in the Palace of Whitehall in London. The portrait is viewed through a hole in a long narrow box, and Hentzner describes it thus: "A picture of King Edward VI representing at first sight something quite deformed, till by looking through a small hole in the cover, which is put over it, you see it in its true proportions." It clearly made quite an impact on people at the time, for William Shakespeare's company, the Lord Chamberlain's Players often played in Whitehall in the 1590s and he must have seen the portrait. In his play *Richard II* (1595-1596), Shakespeare writes:

> "For sorrow's eye, glazed with blinding tears,
> Divides one thing entire to many objects;
> Like perspectives which rightly gaz'd upon,
> Show nothing but confusion—ey'd awry,
> Distinguish form."

William Scrotes?

PRINCE EDWARD

This painting (*below*) dating from 1546 has not only been attributed to Strotes, but also Cornelius Anthonisz, and the Antwerp painter Marc Willems.

ARTISTIC DISTORTIONS

55

HOOGSTRATEN AND BEYOND

Many artists continued to be interested in anamorphosis in the 1600s but only one has left really significant anamorphic works—Samuel van Hoogstraten, the Dutch artist who also created the world's most famous peepshow (*see pp.20-23*). On the lid of his peepshow, for instance, he painted a Venus and Cupid in bed together anamorphically (*below*). By the 1700s, though, perspective was regarded as so easy that no one seems to have been interested in distorting it.

One of the few recent artists to be at all concerned with anamorphosis was Adelbert Ames whose remarkable rooms are in their way anamorphic (*see pp. 16-17*). In the skeletal chairs he also designed, all appear as real chairs when viewed through a peephole. But when the "chairs" are seen fully, you realize that only one is a proper chair; the rest are merely objects arranged to fool the eye in a manner which is really a variant of anamorphosis.

Samuel van Hoogstraten
VENUS AND CUPID

It was common in the 1600s to decorate many boxes with enticing erotic scenes, often taken from classical mythology, to lend an air of respectability. Only Hoogstraten combined it with a display of eyecatching anamorphic art. The need to look on it from just one correct direction adds to the erotic piquancy.

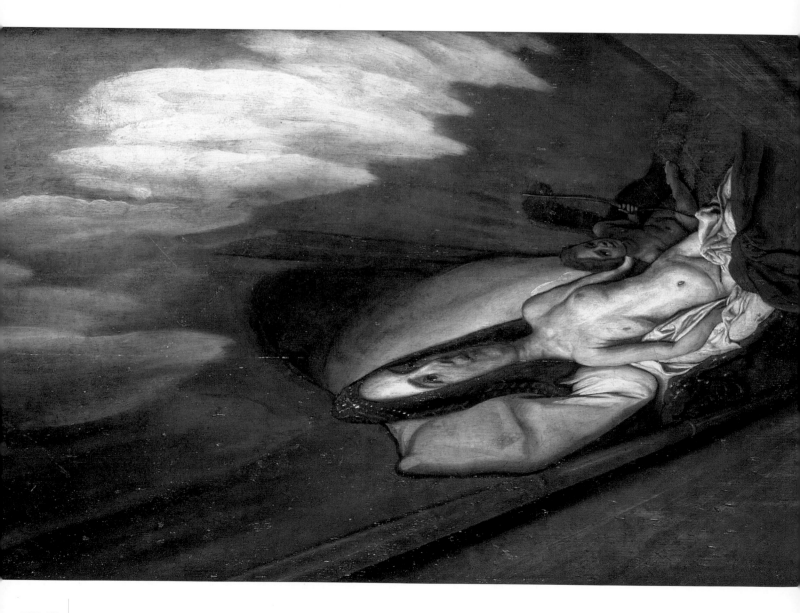

VP

CRAZY REFLECTIONS

Mirrors (*above*), formed into concave or convex shapes, provide an anamorphic, distorted reflection of the viewer.

DISTORTING MIRRORS AND SIGNS

Earlier in this century, anamorphic distortion received a brief revival in the form of crazy mirrors. These mirrors were common attractions in places such as fairgrounds and amusement arcades or even the entrances to stores. Anamorphic concave mirrors show people looking absurdly tall and thin while convex mirrors show them as grotesquely short and fat, with their entire features distorted.

Among the most widely seen examples of anamorphosis today are traffic signs such as POLICE (often on cars) or STOP signs. These are designed to make sense when seen from a speeding car at a distance or in a rearview mirror, rather than when seen fully frontal and stationary (*see pp. 36-37*).

METAMORPHOSING

Besides anamorphic art, there exists a long tradition of "metamorphic art"—art in which particular shapes are deliberately used to create completely different shapes.

Vor zeytten pfiff ich hin vnd her
Aus solchen Pfeiffen dicht vnd mer
Vil Fabel Trewm vnd fanthasey
Ist yetzundt auß vnd gar entzwey
Das ist mir leyd auch schwer vnd bang
Doch hoff ich es wer auch nit lang
Sie weyl die welt so füruitz ist
Sunderlich dückisch vol arger list.

METAMORPHIC ART

The master of metamorphic art was the Italian painter Giuseppe Arcimboldo (1527-1593). For his patron Emperor Rudolf of Austria, Arcimboldo painted extraordinary portraits of people, entirely made up from realistic vegetables and pans (for a cook), books (for a scholar), pieces of armor (for a soldier) and so on. In the 20th century, surrealists such as Dali, hailed him as an early surrealist.

Anonymous

DEVIL WITH BAGPIPES

Dating from the turbulent days of the Lutheran Reformation in Germany, this woodcut (above) shows the devil blowing the bagpipes through a monk's head—implying monks were playing the devil's tune.

Tony Blair (*right*) is morphed with a photo of his wife to become Mrs Tony Blair (*below centre*).

Pamela Anderson (*above*) is morphed with a photo of her husband to create Mr Pamela Anderson

MORPHING

The computerized photographic technique called morphing creates some of the most remarkable metamorphoses to date. A photo of one person is transformed step by step to one of someone else. Photos are converted to computer files by laser scanning. The reflection of laser light from the photo is picked up by a sensor that "reads" the different light levels and gives each a digital code, readable by image-manipulating software. Once the photograph has been digitized, it can be manipulated on screen. Morphing involves moving segments called pixels from one photo image to another to gradually effect a transformation.

Chris Evans (*above*) is morphed with a photo of his wife to create Mrs Chris Evans (*above right*).

CHAPTER 4

IMPOSSIBLE FIGURES

All the best impossible images fool you to begin with—if you want to draw attention to something impossible, it is much more mind-boggling if it is not immediately obvious. A characteristic feature of such impossible objects is that they can only be rendered in black and white: they cannot be colored in. The repeated prongs pattern depicted here has been partly colored in, but it would be impossible to color in the prongs themselves, because they just slip away into nothingness. There is something very slightly irritating about images such as these, which at first appear to be so solid—only to slip away to nothingness before our very eyes.

BAFFLING STRUCTURES

All of the optical illusions described earlier in the book are simply distortions of reality. Our eyes and brain may be deceived by such instances—but once we realize the deception, they make perfect sense. However, there is a whole category of objects which look perfectly ordinary and undistorted—but simply do not make sense.

Impossible figures may not always baffle your eye but they certainly confuse your mind. Even if you do not know much about the laws of geometry, you at once realize, while looking at such objects, that they basically do not add up. Their right angles have more than 90 degrees in them, their parallels are not parallel, lines intersect where they should not. And yet they somehow look convincing. All of this is highly intriguing, sometimes disquieting or even exhilarating—a way of almost seeing extradimensional shapes. For mathematicians, multiple dimensions are routine, yet they can never be constructed in our real framework of height, width and depth.

THE IMPOSSIBLE TRI-BAR

One of the first and best known impossible figures was discovered, more or less by accident, by the Swedish artist Oscar Reutersvärd in 1934. This is the Impossible Tri-bar. Looking at it, your eye immediately accepts it as a triangular three-dimensional figure represented on a two-dimensional surface. But your mind, an instant later, rejects it as logically impossible!

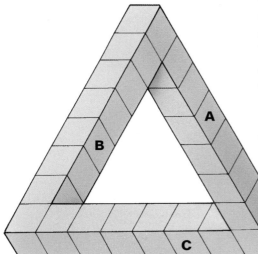

All three sides appear to be perpendicular to each other and to form a neat, closed triangle. But when you add up the sums of their three right-angled corners, you reach a total of 270 degrees—that is, 90 degrees more than is mathematically possible.

Once your eye and mind, working together, have realized that the tri-bar really is impossible, the tri-bar theoretically should either rearrange itself like an ambiguous object (see pp. 38-39), or should dissolve into a meaningless group of lines. Instead it continues to demonstrate a solid presence as a tri-bar to the eye, even though the mind finds its existence unacceptable. Both eye and mind are right; the tri-bar does exist on paper but it does not, indeed cannot, exist in real life. If the tri-bar is deconstructed into numbered sections, there is a strong temptation to try to reassemble them into a logical object. But the attempt remains doomed. It is only possible to construct a model viewable from a very precise angle.

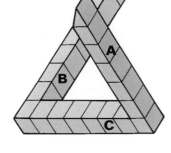

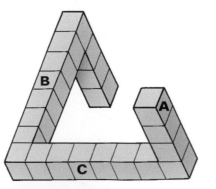

The bar marked C is horizontal while bar A inclines towards us and bar B recedes away into the picture—to meet bar A at the apex. This is clearly preposterous!

WHAT CAN YOU SEE?

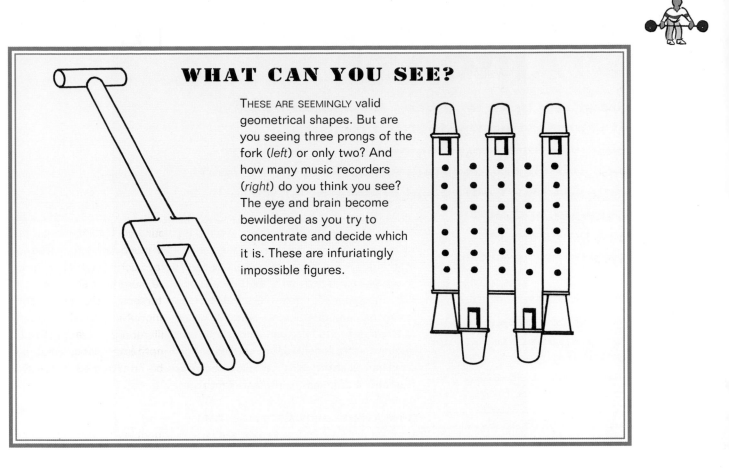

THESE ARE SEEMINGLY valid geometrical shapes. But are you seeing three prongs of the fork (*left*) or only two? And how many music recorders (*right*) do you think you see? The eye and brain become bewildered as you try to concentrate and decide which it is. These are infuriatingly impossible figures.

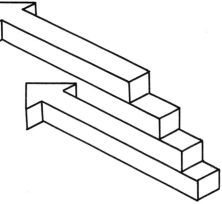

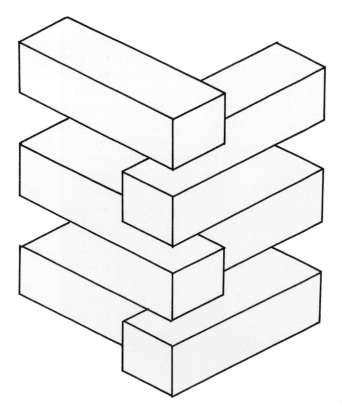

Oscar Reutersvärd

TWO ARROWS
What appear to be two arrows (*above*) have four ends.

LAYERED BLOCKS
Seemingly logical blocks turn out to have highly illogical dimensions which do not add up (*left*).

THE PENROSE STAIRCASE

Scientists have long been fascinated by ways of representing the fourth dimension. Although this has remained an impossibility, two British professors have created something very similar: a perpetual staircase, which leads up and down and up again in a never-ending circle.

HOW IT WORKS: an impossible model

PARADOXICALLY, it is possible to make an *impossible* tribar. Models reveal that pseudo-triangular objects, like the Penroses' triangle, and the Ames Room (*see p. 16*), must be viewed from the "correct" angle to work visually. You can now understand with your intellect how an impossible triangle works. The strangely disquieting point is that when you look again at the triangle from the "correct" angle, it once again convinces your eye that it is a perfectly valid tri-bar, even though your mind knows it is nothing of the sort. It seems as if your eye is forced to choose some likely shape from among those already familiar to it.

In 1958, two British professors of psychology, L. S. Penrose and his son Roger (now one of the world's leading cosmologists) published the first academic paper to try to explain impossible objects. Although they knew nothing of the Swedish artist Oscar Reutersvärd (*see p. 62*), the Penroses were fascinated by Escher's art. In their paper, they said that in impossible figures: "Each individual part is acceptable as a representation of an object normally situated in three-dimensional space; and yet owing to false connections of the parts, acceptance of the whole figure on this basis leads to the illusory effect of an impossible figure."

They illustrated their idea by drawing a triangle similar to Reutersvärd's, and then a more complex triple triangle which baffles the eye so acutely that you have to make a constant effort to focus on it. Finally, they created the famous Penrose Staircase (*below right*).

The Penrose Staircase is one that continually ascends or descends. Each section of this weird staircase seems a reasonable picture of a flight of steps—but the connections between the four sections just do not make sense. The steps seem to be descending forever in a clockwise direction, which is of course impossible.

Roger Penrose went on to make a model of this perpetual staircase. The model, when viewed from the correct angle, gave exactly the same impression as the drawings. He even contrived to photograph it convincingly—although he confessed that the far righthand step was much closer to the camera and higher than the step which seems to be above it. A more complex version of the Penrose Staircase is *Stair Blocks*, also designed by Roger Penrose, in 1958. This combines five impossible cuboids connected by flights of steps. Again, viewed as individual cubes, the stairs make initial sense, but if you tried to follow them around the circuit, you would constantly be switching from a vertical stance to a horizontal one!

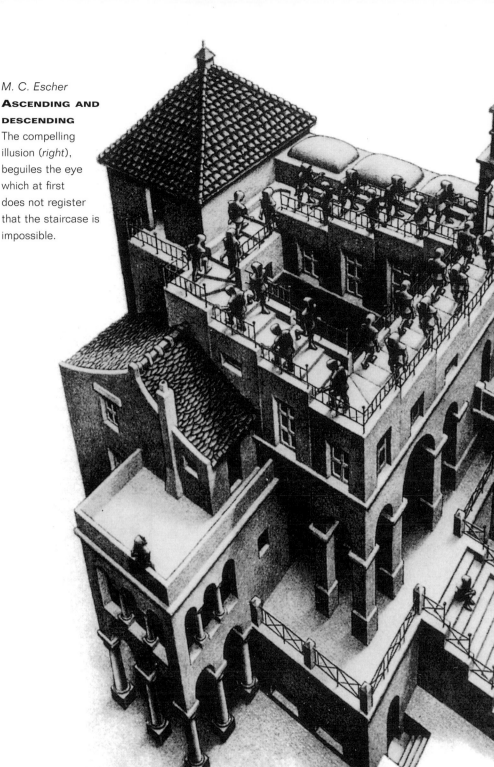

M. C. Escher

ASCENDING AND DESCENDING
The compelling illusion (*right*), beguiles the eye which at first does not register that the staircase is impossible.

HOW IT WORKS:

the Penrose Staircase

The diagram (*right*) simplifies the Penrose Staircase concept to show the structure. Each of the individual steps appears to be roughly the same size. The combination of lines and cubes misleads the eye into recognizing the shapes as something we are familiar with. We incorrectly assume that because we can see the front of the steps they are coming toward us, and the back of the steps travel away from us.

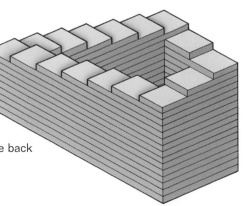

ESCHER'S IMPOSSIBLE TOWER

Many artists this century have become fascinated by impossible objects, especially Escher. Although his interest developed late in life, he created what are probably the most intriguing and certainly the most beautiful of all impossible figures.

ESCHER'S FIRST IMPOSSIBLE OBJECT was his *Cube with Magic Bands* of 1957. You need to look at this cube enclosing circular bands closely before you realize just what exactly is impossible about it.

It is not the skeleton iron cube itself but the bands, which snake around each other and around the diagonal struts in a way which does not quite add up. The band tilting away from the horizontal should be in front of the vertical band, but, remarkably, the two actually seem to merge. Again they seem to twist and change direction in a surprising way because our eyes are mislead by the false shadows Escher has included. The band is possible, but the lighting is not.

In 1958, Escher went on to produce one of his most hauntingly beautiful lithographic works, *Belvédère*.

THE MYSTERIOUS TOWER

At first glance, this appears to represent a mysterious and ancient belvedere or tower in which silent figures, romantically dressed in medieval costume, look out over a magical landscape.

The landscape itself is drawn according to traditional laws of perspective and this helps to deceive your eye, at first anyway, into taking the whole picture at face value. But your mind may notice something illogical about the picture.

The colonnade running round the first or main floor of the tower, with its noble columns supporting a typical Escher-style arched roof, fails to make a logical connection between its upper and lower stories.

You can see this most clearly in the way the ladder rises to the upper floor, where the arches suddenly move from being in the foreground to background. This does not make sense, no matter how you interpret it. The reason is that, at the very center of the picture, Escher has created an impossible but marvellously unobtrusive cuboid (rectangular object). This teases and seduces the eye into thinking it knows exactly what shape everything is—while leaving it entirely baffled.

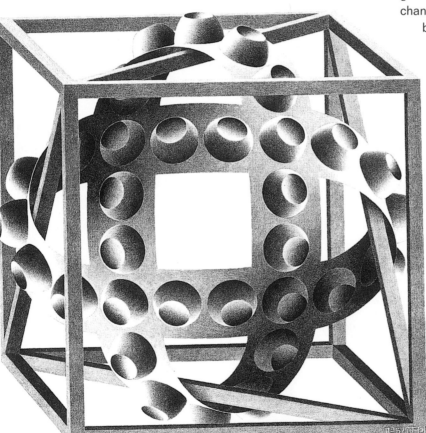

M. C. Escher

CUBE WITH MAGIC BANDS

With this piece, Escher uses our interpretation of shadows to create a frustratingly impossible image. The mind relies so much on what shadows tell us about shape that it is easily deluded by lying shadows. We cannot tell whether the ribbon recedes from view or curves towards us.

HOW IT WORKS: Belvédère

YOU CAN WORK OUT how Escher's Belvédère works by examining the underlying structure. The key to the illusion is misleading perspective clues. The horizontal planes of the cuboid are long and narrow. Escher places parts of the cube which might contradict each other as far apart as possible and takes care to conceal their contradictions. The ceiling, for example, is half-hidden by the arches while the floor is obscured by the balustrade. So Escher can disguise the fact that the upper storey is really at right angles to the lower one. (*see the analysis of Escher's Belvédère below*). The woman on the top floor is gazing in a different direction from the man below, yet both are standing between the same line of columns! For this to work in reality, the columns would have to be highly curved. By his meticulous realism elsewhere, Escher conveys an overall impression of solid reality, thus skillfully camouflaging this great contradiction at the core.

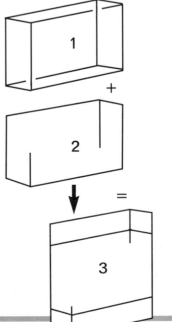

PERPETUAL MOTION

The concept of perpetual motion—has challenged scientists since the Renaissance. Artists like M. C. Escher appear to depict it in their work...but appearances can be deceptive.

M. C. Escher

WATERFALL

Escher's artistic detail beguiles the eye into believing the structure (*right*) is viable.

Soon after creating his impossible *Belvédère* (*see p. 67*), M. C. Escher came to hear of the Penrose Staircase (*see pp.64-65*). He wrote the Penroses a letter in April 1960, saying he was so taken with their concept of a "continuous staircase" that he had been inspired to create one himself.

In his *Ascending and Descending*, Escher created a haunting image. At the top of a typically fantastic house, men as mindless as automatons trudge round and round steps which seem to be constantly descending. Although visually bewildering, however, this should not be classified as a fully impossible object. It might just be feasible to create such a house by angling the stairs very carefully in a different way on each side. The following year, however, inspired by his correspondence with the Penroses, Escher created a truly and absolutely impossible building.

Waterfall is both geometrically and physically impossible yet it looks remarkably convincing. The clever construction, along with Escher's artistic detail, makes it particularly realistic. Water flows steadily in its channels uphill round a circuit, under the towers, until it cascades down and turns a waterwheel. This in turn propels the water on its way up the course—a circular energy system which defies the laws of physics! The secret ideal of so many medieval philosophers, *perpetuum mobile*—or perpetual, self-generating motion—here appears to have been fulfilled. But appearances once again deceive.

The self-filling waterfall is by no means the only impossibility in the picture. If you look closely you will see that, although it is composed of square beams resting on each other at right angles, the water channel follows an impossible course, turning sharp left under the right hand tower before turning back under the same tower a level higher. The two towers are obviously of the same height, but the lefthand one has an extra storey. Concealed within the picture are at least three impossible tri-bars.

Escher explored another illusional avenue with his version of a *Möbius Strip (left)* in which ants crawl round the twisted band in a never-ending cycle. Möbius strips are not illusions but real objects created by twisting a strip of paper through 180 degrees and joining the ends. They have the curious property of converting a two-sided sheet of paper into a shape with just one continuous surface. You can prove this by drawing a line down the middle of both sides of the strip without lifting the pen from the paper to turn over.

M. C. Escher

MÖBIUS STRIP

The ants' endless cycle (*above*) emphasizes the one-sidedness of the band.

HOW IT WORKS: waterfall

THE ARTIST SHIGEO FUKUDA made an actual model (*left*) of M. C. Escher's *Waterfall*. As with the tri-bar, it worked visually when seen from one "correct" angle, but viewed otherwise it fell apart—into a meaningless mess of drunken looking towers leaning at crazy angles with wide gaps in the structure.

IMPOSSIBLE OBJECTS

When the possible has been achieved, all too perfectly and seemingly all too easily, try the impossible! Such seems to have been the motto of some artists, who delight in their impossible creations.

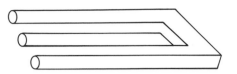

Many artists and scientists around the world have independently created similar impossible figures. The Swedish artist Oscar Reutersvärd drew some almost annoyingly impossible three-barred figures, which tease both the eye and mind. Sandro del Prete has drawn a three-barred candlestick, the middle candle of which disappears beneath its flame, while the square base of the righthand candle is strangely lost in the background toward its top.

Del Prete has also invented a remarkable new type of flywheel, which he calls *The Quadrature of the Wheel* (*below*). With it are plans supposedly showing the principles behind this squared wheel, with the individual components on the left and a frontal view of the axle on the right. You may not be convinced by these plans, however, and you would be right. Although the six beams of the outer frame are possible enough, the four spokes could never fit into them. Instead, they would stick right out of the "wheel". It is a truly impossible figure.

Bruno Ernst, who has made a lifetime study of impossible art, has also created many classically impossible figures. Among them are impossible triangles awkwardly caged in a room (*left*) and *Collage* which cunningly combines an impossible crossbar with a traditional landscape to make a doubly disconcerting painting.

Another effective impossible figure is Zenon Kulpa's two-and-a half dimensional *1=2*, which at first sight seems disconcertingly simple—two bars with a long shadow beside them. But are you seeing two bars or only one? The eye and brain become bewildered as you try to concentrate and decide which it is. This is an infuriatingly impossible figure.

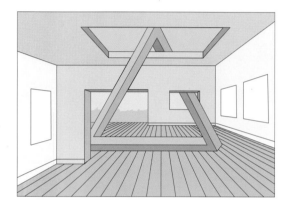

Bruno Ernst
IMPOSSIBLE TRI-BAR IN IMPOSSIBLE ROOM
Ernst's impossible tri-bar is caged in a room with the tip of the tri-bar obscured by the ceiling.

HOW IT WORKS: Quadrature of the Wheel

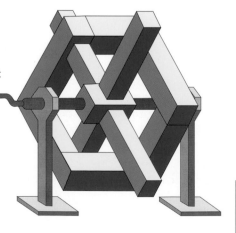

Sandro del Prete
QUADRATURE OF THE WHEEL
THE SIX BEAMS composing the outer wheel rim are not impossible. However, on closer examination of the axles, one can see this wheel could not possibly ever move round or rotate—as first appears!

IMPOSSIBLE FIGURES IN HISTORY

Before the discovery of perspective in the Renaissance, many artists painted what at first sight seem to be impossible figures. In fact, very few artists were concerned with creating possible figures at all. Scale, distance and perspective are all distorted as many medieval paintings show. But these paintings are not really impossible figures in the true sense because they are not visually logical in the way that figures like the tri-bar are (*see p. 62*). In other words we could never be taken in and believe they were accurate pictures of reality. Medieval artists had just not worked out how to, or simply were not interested in trying to, show things in true perspective.

Probably the first deliberately impossible painting was that by the Dutch artist Pieter Breughel (1525-69), one of the greatest Renaissance painters of northern Europe. In *The Magpie on the Gallows* (*above*), Breughel seems to have been unique as an impossible artist both in his lifetime and for many generations afterwards.

Pieter Breughel

THE MAGPIE ON THE GALLOWS

The peasants looking on at the impossibly twisted four-bar gallows have every reason to be alarmed. Such an object cannot, should not, exist.

PIRANESI'S MONUMENTS

One of the forerunners of the Romantic Revolution in art was the Venetian artist Giovanni Battista Piranesi, whose nightmarish imaginary prisons thrilled the world in the mid 1700s.

Piranesi (1720-1778) was one of the greatest creators of fantastic and highly romantic interiors. His drawings also, perhaps unintentionally, broke the laws of perspective to become impossible. Piranesi started his career as an architect, but he is best known for his series of remarkable engravings, *Carceri d'Invenzione* (*Imaginary Prisons*). First published in 1745, these were revised, made yet more extraordinary, and republished in 1760. Going far beyond the customary gentle and nostalgic depictions of ruined classical buildings, they are among the first and most significant harbingers of the new Romantic Movement which was about to sweep across the world. Appropriately, among his engravings Piranesi included some views which seem to undermine the classical Renaissance ideas of perspective.

IN PERPETUITY

In his *Carceri*, gigantic arches rise above sinister, deep abysses, huge flights of stairs climb from the shadows to end nowhere, great wheels suggesting hideous tortures emerge from the darkness, and all human beings are dwarfed.

In his most dramatic engravings, Piranesi begins to transcend the customary three dimensions. The brooding massiveness of the architecture with its threatening shadows nearly obscures the fact that there is something very odd going on with the architecture here. If you look closely, you will see that the wall in the background, with its three tall Gothic arches, starts off logically enough on the left. However, the central arch seems to move into the foreground in its lower section, becoming part of the series of three rounded arches in the center foreground. The staircase itself starts by running parallel to this massive wall but then moves imperceptibly behind it.

Giovanni Battista Piranesi
CARCERI VII, 1745
Even in early, more realistic engravings (*above*), Piranesi imagined scenes that were nightmarishly oppressive — and almost impossible.

HOW IT WORKS: imaginary prisons

IN SKELETON DIAGRAMS FOR Piranesi's great work, you can see far more clearly how the arched wall moves forward in its central column towards the front of the picture. At the same time the staircase seems to change plane as it changes direction, ducking behind the middle pillar. How far Piranesi was aware of what he was doing is unknown.

Marcel Duchamp

APOLLINÈRE ENAMELED, 1916-17

By removing one bar from the bed, Duchamp has turned an innocent normal poster bed into a witty master-piece of impossible art. The eye is tricked into seeing what is not there.

intensify the atmosphere of proto-Romantic horror. But, whether or not he was aware of it, he did create multiple planes in a way which is truly baffling for the observer.

DUCHAMP'S TRIBUTE

Marcel Duchamp (1887-1968) was one of the most influential theorists and artists of this century. He was a believer in the absurdity and the futility of everything, especially art, and a pioneer in impossible figures, as his picture, *Apollinère Enameled* reveals. This was intended as a humorous tribute to his friend, the poet and art critic Guillaume Apollinaire (1880-1918). He transformed an advertisement for Sapolin, a well known brand of paint, by changing and adding certain letters. He also made a bed into an archetypal impossible figure by seeming to join the farther horizontal bar with the end of the bedstead and extending the vertical of the head of the bed with the frame.

IMPROBABLE FIGURES

There is a further kind of impossible figure—or perhaps more appropriately—"Improbable Figures", which are essentially wildly imaginative works. They shock the viewer by adding impossible elements to everyday objects. A typical example is *Spiked Iron* by the great American Surrealist photographer, sculptor, and movie maker Man Ray (1890-1977).

CUBISM: AN IMPOSSIBLE ART?

By the early 1900s many younger artists were beginning to abandon the fixed rules of perspective and realistic images. Partly driven by the proof that photographs could reproduce reality perfectly adequately, they began to search for new ways of depicting things, building images up in terms of cubes (Cubism), or even completely abstractly.

Unlike more conventional art forms, Cubism cannot be taught, yet it is a highly intellectual school. Cubist paintings recall reality, but the objects are impossible. In a painting such as Braque's *Houses at l'Estaque* (*right*), there is no proper horizon, no real vanishing point and no real perspective. Instead, solid blocks of simply drawn houses heave themselves out of the canvas towards you, in a way that threatens to become four-dimensional. The fourth dimension is not time, but the ability to see the opposite sides of an object simultaneously. Picasso achieved this effect in his *Seated Nude* (1910), in which it seems as though we are seeing the figure from different viewpoints.

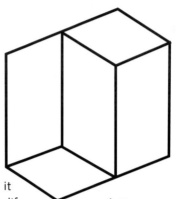

1 ELEMENTS OF CUBISM
Just as Thiery's Cube (*above*) constantly reverses so you cannot be sure which is solid and which void, so a Cubist picture seems to extend out of the canvas toward you.

2 UPFRONT EXTENSION
The stacked elements (*left*), lit from no clearly defined source, not only make our position in relation to the houses uncertain, but give the impression that they are marching out of the painting toward us.

3 BACK TO FRONT
Instead of working in to the painting, using perspective to suggest depth, Braque worked from the background (*right*) forward, making each element within it clearly defined—rather than fudged by distance. The lack of horizon further confuses the viewer's interpretation of pictorial space.

CHAPTER 5

APPARENT MOVEMENT

So far we have only looked at stable or static illusions but we live in a world in constant motion. Many movements, such as the molecular change within your own body or in a table, are too slow to notice. Others, like a bullet shattering an apple, happen too fast for your eyes, or most normal cameras, to register. But between those two extremes lies much of the everyday world, a world governed by movement. The turning of wheels or propellers, the flashing on-off of advertisement signs, the passing of cars or of people—all are vital parts of life. In many ways, movement *is* life.

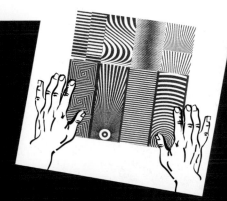

ADJUSTING TO SPEED

Just as our eyes can be fooled by misleading signs in static images, so they can be fooled by movement. Some movement, like the shattering of a light bulb, is simply too fast for our eyes to register. Some, like the growing of a plant, is too slow. There are other movements that we see, but see wrongly, or in a particular way, that create optical illusions.

MICHAEL FARADAY demonstrated how the persistence of vision worked.

There is a limit to how fast the eye can send signals to the brain. This is because the light-sensitive cells in the retina do not stop sending signals to the brain the instant the scene changes. Instead, they carry on sending them for a fraction of a second. This is called retinal lag and means the eye can register a new picture no more frequently than every sixteenth of a second or so.

The result is that very rapid movement becomes blurred, as separate but similar images appear to merge into each other. Your eye and brain in effect read fast-moving objects not as a series of distinct "snapshots" but as a continuous flow. You can see this for yourself by spinning a bicycle wheel gradually faster. At first you see the individual spokes as they go round, but as the wheel gains speed, the spokes begin to blur.

Psychologists call this process persistence of vision. It was first observed by Leonardo da Vinci in the days of the Renaissance, and first demonstrated clearly by the British scientist Michael Faraday (1791-1867) in 1825 with a very simple experiment (*left*). He cut a small slice in a paperboard disk, mounted it on a bent paperclip shaft and spun it. While the disk was in motion, it became virtually invisible; you could see everything behind it. One effect of this phenomenon is that if still "snapshots" change rapidly enough they blur into one another to create an illusion of continuous movement. You can see this for yourself by flipping the pages at the top of the book very fast. The images in the corner appear to come to life and move. Of course they do not, but your eye is deceived by the swiftly changing pictures. This is called serial transformation and is the basis of all animation—and indeed for all movies.

FARADAY'S VISION

Cut a narrow slit in a lightweight paperboard circle and spin it on a shaft made from a bent paperclip to see "persistence of vision".

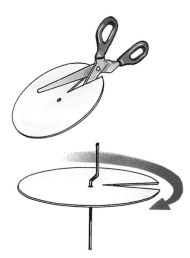

HIGH SPEED VISION

A high speed train becomes a blur to our eyes which are unable to cope with such rapidity.

WHAT IS MOVING?

You judge movement by comparing it with things that appear to be still. You can see how fast a car is moving, for instance, by comparing it with the still background of the houses behind. In the same way, if you are moving, you judge your movement in relation to things you are passing. This comparison of movement to a still background is called motion parallax.

This mechanism means that when you move your head, the brain so easily recognizes that it is your head that is moving that the view in front of you appears still, as it should. Every now and then, however, the brain can be fooled. When an apparently still background begins to move, your brain may give you a dizzying sensation that it is you that is moving. This can often happen when you are sitting in a station and the train next to yours pulls out—giving you a powerful impression that you are moving backward. You have to check which is actually moving: your vehicle or the other.

At slow speeds, we hardly notice motion parallax but it becomes much more pronounced in a fast-moving car. Speeding through wooded areas, for example, you may experience a dizzying, flickering succession of tree trunks whizzing past, as your eyes fail to adjust quickly enough to the motion. By contrast, if you are moving across wide open spaces such as prairies or deserts, nearby objects such as road signs shoot past rapidly but far distant mountains appear to remain stable for long periods, and the moon remains completely immobile.

A recent new discovery has been made in France by passengers on the TGV, the very fast trains which can travel at more than 200 km/h (125 mph). Distant cloud formations, which in reality are stable, appear to swirl around. Although airplanes go far faster, they normally fly much higher so this phenomenon has not been observed from them.

MOVEMENT IN ART

Until the invention of the movie just over a century ago, artists had little hope of recording or representing rapid movement accurately. Instead, they had to try and create the illusion of movement in a single, still image.

Some movements are simply too fast for an artist to analyze accurately. There is a famous statue of the Roman Emperor Marcus Aurelius on the Capitoline Hill in Rome. The seated Emperor looks realistic enough but his cantering horse seems oddly stiff and unreal. The sculptor has not caught the essence of its movement at all.

In the 1600s, Baroque art, with its love of dynamic curves and melodrama, encouraged new attempts to represent movement in art. *The Fall of the Damned*, by the great Flemish painter Peter Paul Rubens (1577-1640), conveys an impression of movement brilliantly with its cascade of human bodies hurtling towards Hell. The impression, however, is more in your mind than your eye. Your mind supplies the next phase of the descent of the damned, in what is termed directed tension. But the picture itself, for all its

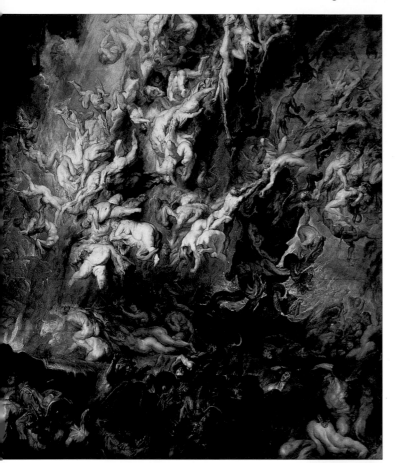

Peter Paul Rubens
THE FALL OF THE DAMNED
The exuberant energies of Rubens, one of the most dynamic Baroque painters, conveys an impression of movement in a single image through this avalanche of bodies tumbling one after another into the abyss.

DID YOU KNOW?

Moving lights

IF YOU WATCH TWO LIGHTS flashing alternately close to each other in a dark room, you see them as a single light moving from one position to another. You do not see them as separate lights because you do not have a still background to compare them to. This phenomenon of apparent movement is called stroboscopic movement and explains why you see flashing neon signs as continuous movement rather than as a series of separate lights going on or off.

Similarly, try putting a flashlight in a cardboard box with a hole in it and place it some distance away. After a while, the light will appear to move, even though it remains stationary. Again, your eye is disorientated by the lack of a still background.

NEON LIGHTS
The phenomenon of stroboscopic movement is seen in the neon lights of Las Vegas. The wave of the cowboy gives the illusion of continuous movement, when, in reality, it is a series of separate lights going on and off.

energy, remains a snapshot of frozen motion, not an actual depiction of movements.

Artists were well aware of this limitation. The Dutch painter Philip Angel wrote in the 1600s, "Whenever a cart wheel or a spinning wheel is turned with great force, you will notice that because of the rapid turning no spokes can really be seen but only an uncertain glimpse of them. Though I have seen many cart wheels represented, I have never yet seen this as it should appear because every spoke is always drawn as if the carriage did not appear to move." Only one or two great artists, such as Diego Vélazquez (1599-1660) managed to paint what we actually see as movement, as in the spinning wheel of *Hilanderas*.

FREEZING MOVEMENT

Early photographic materials were so insensitive that subjects had to remain perfectly still for long periods for the picture to be sharp. But by the 1870s, they had improved enough to register even quite fast movement. In 1872, the photographer Edward Muybridge (1830-1904) was asked in 1872 by the railroad magnate Leland Stanford to photograph a horse in motion.

The idea was to settle both a bet and a question which had bothered artists for centuries: did a galloping horse ever have all four legs in the air at the same moment? Ingeniously, Muybridge set up a battery of 17 cameras with high-speed shutters that would be triggered by the horse as it went by. In this way, he took a series of photographs that showed horses do have all four legs tucked under them as they gallop!

Muybridge went on to photograph humans and other animals with his timed cameras, showing his pictures to scientific bodies all over the U. S. and Europe.

At about the same time, around 1882, a Frenchman, Emile Reynaud, was charming audiences in Paris with his Praxinoscope, one of several contemporary attempts to project moving images. His Praxinoscope employed a rotating drum which used mirrors and a lantern to project cartoons onto a screen. The effect was jerky and slow and it was hard work making all the cartoons by hand.

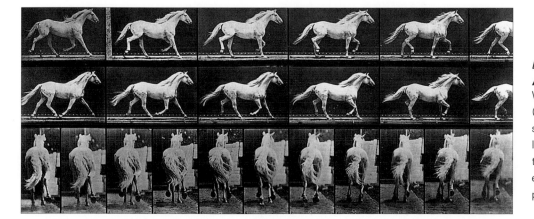

Edward Muybridge
ANIMAL LOCOMOTION
When a horse is galloping (*left*), there is, in reality, no single point when all four legs are off the ground—this is still hard to believe, even though it has been proven here to be true!

THE COMING OF THE MOVIES

Nothing is more illusory than the movies—not just in the scenes and characters they show but also, even more crucially, in the way they show them. For movie images never in fact move at all: they only appear to move, in an illusion so powerful that it is easily overlooked.

MOVIE PIONEER
Louis Lumière (*below*), who with his brother Auguste, invented the movies, examining a reel of movie film—a frame of static shots which ran at high speed to depict movement.

On March 22, 1895 the brothers Louis and Auguste Lumière demonstrated to a select audience in Paris the world's first true moving picture, prosaically titled *Workers Leaving the Factory*. Like all movies, their film relied on persistence of vision (see p. 116) to create a moving image. They used a small portable camera able to take 16 separate pictures every second by running a long strip of 35 mm wide film rapidly past the lens. Their remarkable camera could be used in conjunction with a powerful light source to project the film at the same speed onto a blank screen. Persistence of vision meant that the rapidly changing, still images gave the illusion of continuous movement.

Many other people, including the great American inventor Thomas Edison (1847-1931), had been working along broadly similar lines. But the Lumière brothers' invention proved the model for movie-making for over a quarter of a century. Within a few years emulators and rivals had started making and showing movies around the world.

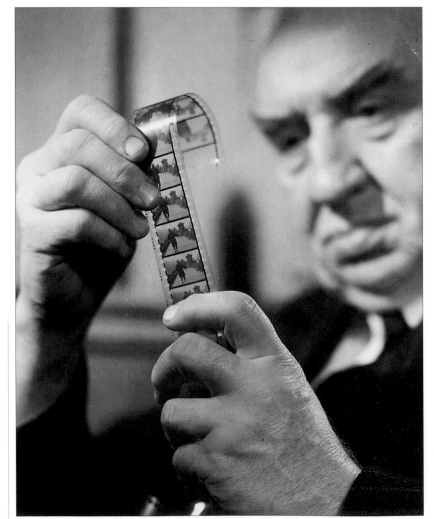

HOW IT WORKS: frames per second

THE LUMIÈRES' INVENTION relied, like all movies, on serial transformation—the same phenomenon at work with the simple animation created by flicking the top of the pages of this book. The brothers chose their speed of 16 frames per second for technical reasons. At faster speeds, the film of the day threatened to snap, as Edison discovered when he experimented with a speed of 44 frames per second. But 16 frames a second is not quite fast enough to fool the eye entirely. As a result, early movies appear somewhat jerky and awkward, at least to our modern eyes, used to films that move at 24 frames a second. Early movies run smoothly if shown at 24 frames per second but figures appear comically speeded up.

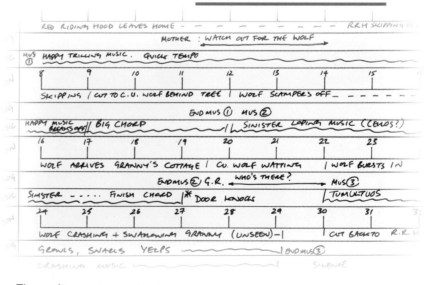

SOUND AND VISION

Al "you ain't heard nothing yet" Jolson in *The Jazz Singer*, the movie of 1927 which synchronized sound and movement.

SYNCHRONIZING SOUND AND MOVEMENT

When you go to the movies, you experience another very powerful illusion. The voices seem to be coming from the mouths of the characters shown on screen in front of you, just as gunfire seems to come from the barrel of a smoking gun and the sound of an automobile engine comes from the car. Unless you are seated in the very front row, you are unlikely ever to notice that in fact the sound is really coming from banks of speakers sited (often invisibly) on either side of the screen.

Early movies were always silent, but by the 1920s, rival systems of adding sound to movies were under development in the three main centers of movie making—Germany, Russia, and the U.S. It was an American system—sound-on-film—which finally won the day. But the first famous "talkie", *The Jazz Singer* of 1927, in which Al Jolson made cinema history by saying, "You ain't heard nothing yet," used a different system: Vitaphone. This consisted of huge phonographic discs, nearly 2 feet (60 cm) across, which were attached to the film projector and produced sound synchronized to the movie. These discs were easier to record on and at first gave better quality sound, but they were cumbersome and broke easily, and were soon superseded by sound-on-film.

The sound-on-film process converts sound into light waves which are reproduced on a photographic stripe running alongside the images on a normal 35 mm film strip. This allows perfect synchronization, so that even if, for example, the film breaks during a performance and has to be repaired, sound and film synchronization is never lost.

DID YOU KNOW: Special effects

THE MOVIES have always used special effects to create illusions, from the rubber models of *King Kong* to the front projections that made superman fly. But in recent years two advances have dramatically advanced the sophistication of special effects—computer manipulation and animatronics—especially in the hands of units like Industrial Light and Magic. Computer programs give film-makers phenomenal power to manipulate the image. Actors, for instance, can be stretched, twisted, squashed, flattened out, blown up or even morphed to someone else—just like cartoon characters used to be. Animatronics is the use of animation models controlled by sophisticated electronics. This is what enabled Spielberg to bring dinosaurs frighteningly to life for his Jurassic Park movies.

GETTING IT TOGETHER

Both action and dialogue are synchronized (*above*)—creating the illusion that the voice is coming out of the mouths of the movie characters—this, in reality, is not the case!

CARTOONS

The word "cartoon" originally meant a large-scale preparatory drawing for a permanent painting or fresco. But in the 1800s the word was applied to satirical drawings in magazines like Punch or The New Yorker. Then, early in the present century cartoons became synonymous with a series of drawings featuring "cartoon" characters. Now the word belongs to the animated movies.

Cartoon animation long predates the Lumière brothers' first movie (*see p. 82*). Throughout the 1800s, households were charmed by the moving images of devices like the zoetrope. This was simply an illuminated drum with slots and a series of pictures on the inside. As the drum spun, the pictures seen through the slots seemed to move. However, it was only with the coming of the movies and high speed film projection that cartoon animation came into its own. Cartoon movies depended on making thousands of separate drawings and then photographing them, frame by frame, on movie film. When projected at 24 frames a second, the images in the drawings appeared to move smoothly.

The undoubted genius of movie cartoons was Walt Disney (1901-1966). Starting with his first Mickey Mouse cartoon *Plane Crazy* in 1928, Disney created a string of brilliant, feature-length films, such as *Snow White and the Seven Dwarfs* (1938) and *Sleeping Beauty* (1959). One of the first movie producers to realize fully the potential of sound, he also combined great music with a carnival ballet of animals in *Fantasia* (1940).

The remarkable quality of Disney's animated films, with their atmospheric landscapes or truly vertiginous skyscrapers, was no accident. Disney employed whole studios of devoted craftsmen to painstakingly create each frame of the cartoons. Since his death, some observers have seen a decline in such illusionistic brilliance, as computer-generated graphics have replaced the traditional artists. The juxtaposing of real human and cartoon characters in films such as *Mary Poppins* and *Who Framed Roger Rabbit?* however, represents a blurring of the frontiers between total illusion and partial reality.

ACTION CAT
Individual frames from MGM's cartoon classic *Tom and Jerry*.

An aperture grille behind the screen lines up with the phosphor stripes on the screen, allowing each color beam to strike only the right color stripes.

The heart of a TV is the tube—a vacuum sealed in a glass bulb.

There are three electron guns at the back of the tube, one for each primary color—red, green and blue.

The picture is created as magnets in the electron guns bend the electron streams to scan rapidly back and forth across the screen.

The back of the screen is coated with stripes of phosphors, alternating red, green and blue. These glow when they are hit by electrons.

GLOWING POINTS

A "gun" (below) at the back of the television creates the picture by firing streams of electrons at the screen to make different parts of it glow intermittently—so that the eye is fooled fast into seeing all the glowing points as a complete, ever-changing picture.

TELEVISION LINES

Unlike movies, television does not rely on projecting a series of still frames to create the illusion of movement. Instead, it works by projecting the image in a series of fluctuating horizontal lines on the television screen. Three electronic scanning guns in the back of the television tube fire fluctuating intensities of voltage (the picture signal) at the screen, which briefly glows with varying degrees of brightness. Every 1/60 second these guns scan 262.5 horizontal lines alternately. The glowing of the screen seems more or less constant because of your persistence of vision (see p. 116) and because the images have few high-contrast edges and are constantly changing.

Although television appears to resemble photography, it is quite different. Photography uses light to trigger simple chemical reactions on a piece of film. Television images consist of a whole series of trans-formations in energy forms (called transductions) before the image arrives on your screen. In fact, a television image is coarse and grainy compared to most photographs and puts a greater strain on your eyes. While watching television, your brain activity also changes, and you often drift into a state of near-drowsiness—one reason why dramatic, often violent, action, and very short scenes are common features.

DID YOU KNOW?

Timelapse photography

IN TIMELAPSE photography, rapid film exposures are made at regular, timed intervals of minutes, hours, or even days— normally of natural objects such as plants, flowers, or even clouds. When shown at normal film speed, this creates the illusion of movement in objects which usually look motionless. Flowers burst into blossom and then quickly fade away and clouds form and dissolve with amazing speed.

MODERN ART AND MOVEMENT

In the modern age, when all types of artistic realism seem outmoded, artists have turned to other forms of illusions. These may in some ways be more clearly apparent but they baffle your eye and brain powerfully with their illusory movements.

With the advent first of photography and then of motion pictures, artists grew less concerned with recording the reality of movement. But in the 1960s, the Op Art (short for Optical Art) movement began to experiment with pictures that stimulated the brain in such a way that they appeared to move. Artists like Bridget Riley (b. 1931) and Victor Vasarely (b. 1908) dazzled the eyes of the art world with startling geometric shapes. Vasarely pioneered his almost hallucinatory style with pictures which seem to be endlessly shifting and changing as in *Zett Zk*. Bridget Riley's pictures are even more disquieting. Looking at them, your eye becomes totally bewildered, trying to read into them forms which are not actually there. Probably your retinal circuits are suffering a sort of overload. When you look away, your eyesight may flicker like a faulty television set.

Bridget Riley
FALL
The simple geometric lines spiralling downwards give the illusion of "falling"—created also by the waves growing progressively larger as they cascade downwards.

HOW IT WORKS:

make the wheels move

MAKE THESE WHEELS move using the acetate sheet provided. Draw the sheet over the printed images and watch them rotate. The printed images on the page consist of fairly regularly spaced black and white areas. The acetate sheet has regularly spaced horizontal lines. When the acetate sheet is drawn across the image on the page, sometimes the horizontal lines block out the white spaces. Sometimes they merge with the black parts of the printed page revealing the white spaces. The dynamic effect is similar to the shifting patterns of light seen on moiré silk.

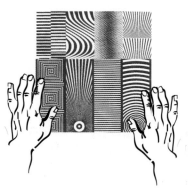

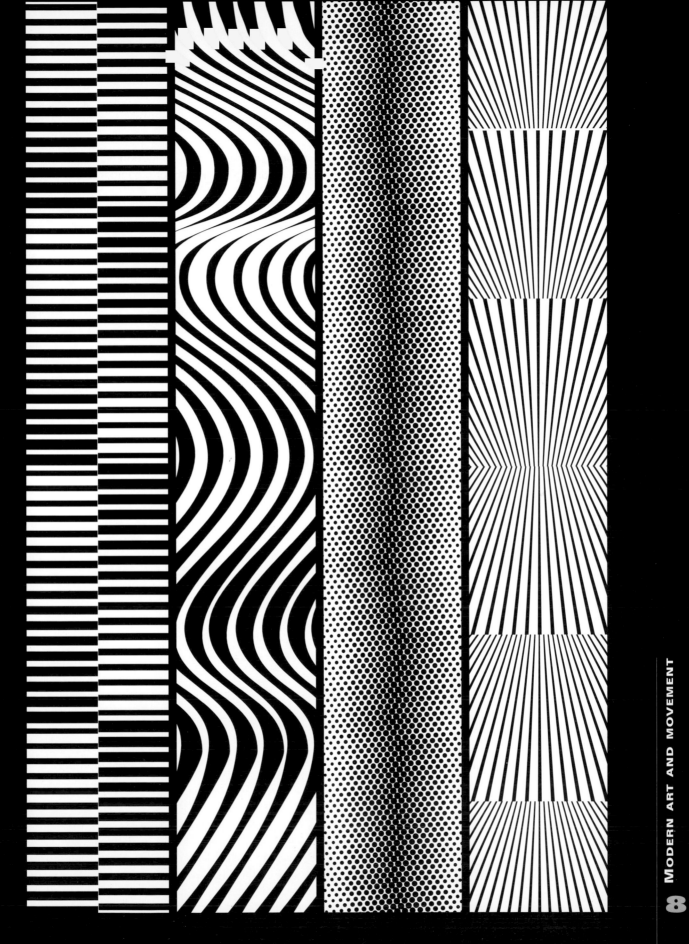

CAMOUFLAGE

Camouflage is not just a response of armies and navies to the changing warfare of the twentieth century. It has been used for disguise in the natural world ever since predators developed eyes to chase prey.

SPOT THE DOG

One of the most famous illusory images is the photograph (*right*) of a dalmatian. Its dark spots and pale patches so perfectly match the dappled background that it is hard to even see there is a dog here at first. The reason is that your eye does not at first see complete shapes, but retinal images made of patterns of light and dark which the brain tries to make sense of. With no strong outlines, the brain has nothing to help it make judgements and so the brain is left confused and the dog invisible.

MILITARY DISGUISES

Once military uniforms were as splendid and bright as possible to make the maximum possible impact. But during the American War of Independence, some British soldiers realized that their bright red uniforms made them all too obvious targets for American marksmen. So they began wearing dull brown buckskins like their opponents. A century later, British troops fighting in the dust of Afghanistan began to swap their bright red and white uniforms for khaki (the Urdu word for dust) and veterans stained their white helmets with tea.

During the twentieth century, all armies have adopted drab camouflage colors for all active service. In the First World War (1914-18), guns, trucks and military installations were disguised with camouflage netting, often covered with leaves, to hide them from aircraft. During the Second World War, the process went further as whole armies tried to vanish. The upper surfaces of fighter planes were painted green and brown to hide them against the ground from overhead aircraft while their undersides were painted pale blue or white to disguise them from below, against the sky. To deceive night-flying enemy bombers, canals were coated in coaldust to reduce reflections.

DRESSED TO KILL

British Army 81mm mortar team (*above*) wearing modern camouflaged battle dress.

NATURAL CAMOUFLAGE

Both hunter and hunted use camouflage to avoid being seen—and increase their chances of making a kill, or staying alive. A cheetah's spots keep it invisible against the dappled shadows of its environment until it is too late for a victim to escape its devastating burst of speed. Woodland birds are dappled brown to help them blend in with the woodland floor and hide them from the prying eyes of hawks. Some animals, such as the stoat and the Arctic Fox, change their color with the seasons, donning a coat of white to blend into the snowscape of the Arctic winter.

CHANGE OF SKIN

Camouflage works in different ways. Some animals adopt background color; others have dark backs and light undersides to counteract the effect of the shadows they would cast in normal light—an effect known as "countershading". The chameleon may actually change the color of its skin to match its background. Some creatures escape detection by mimicking some aspect of their environment which their predators would find inedible—like the Sphinx Moth caterpillar which looks like a twig encrusted with fungus. Others depend on breaking up the outline by which we normally recognize shapes—an effect called "disruptive coloration". The strong stripes of the tiger are so marked that eyes see them just as shadows in the grass rather than as the threatening outline of the animal.

A PERFECT MATCH

The narrow-headed tree frog (*above*) from the Amazonian jungle matches its background perfectly—its first line of defence against detection or attack.

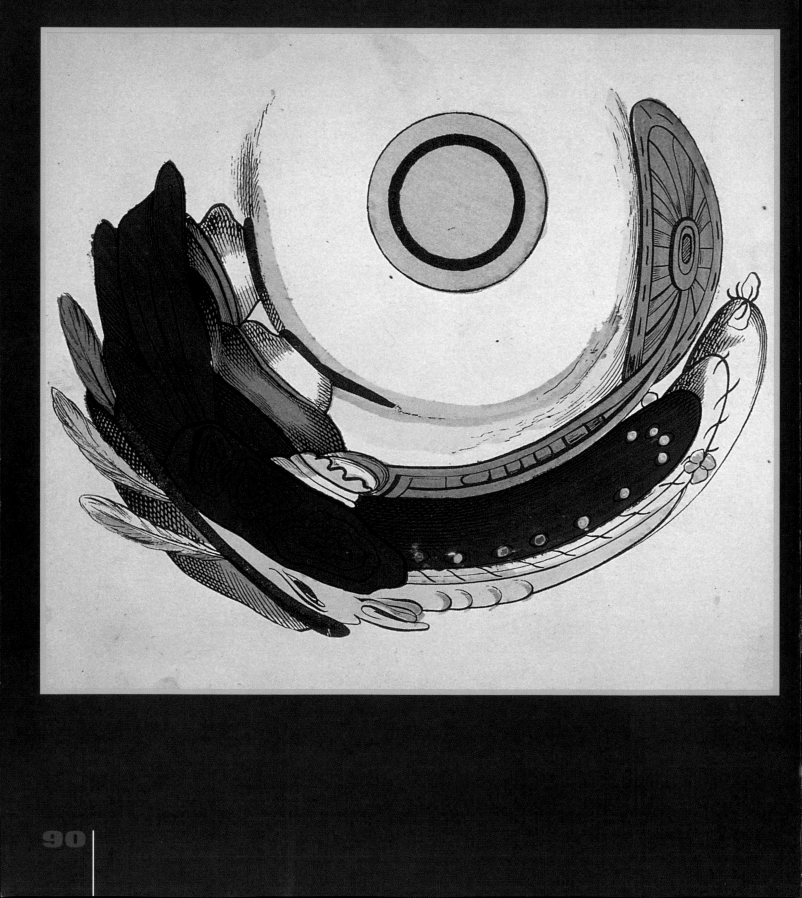

CHAPTER 6

STEREOSCOPY

Anamorphosis—from the Greek
meaning "transform shape"—has
come to refer to a picture or part of a
picture that gives a markedly distorted
image of the object represented...unless
it is seen from a particular
angle or through a special
lens or mirror, when it is
transformed into its true
form. Curve the silver
sheet supplied with this
book to see the reflection
of the images on this
page revealed.

STEREOSCOPIC VISION

Each eye gives us a slightly different view; the nearer the subject, the greater the difference. The brain combines the different views to give us "stereoscopic vision" which enables us to judge shape, distance, depth, and dimension with ease.

CYLINDRICAL ANAMORPHOSIS

It is easier to make optical toys for one eye than two, because the second eye provides a second point-of-view. This anamorphic image inside a foil roll (*see also pp. 90-1*) works only with one eye.

What is extraordinary about our two-eyed, "binocular" vision is that we still have the powerful sensation that we are looking through just one big eye in the middle of our heads—not two small ones on either side. This is sometimes called the Cyclops Syndrome after the Cyclops of ancient Greek mythology—giants, notoriously gifted with immense strength, dangerously bad tempers...and one allseeing eye in the middle of their foreheads.

Your brain normally processes its two retinal images so that you experience them as one image through what is termed image fusion. Each eye has a marginally different visual field (which is termed binocular disparity) but the images are generally similar and overlap.

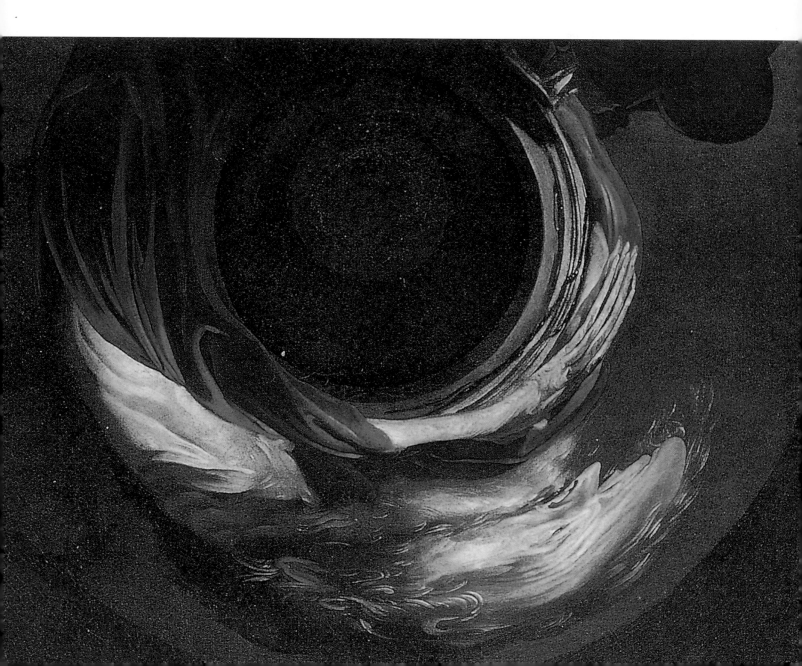

DOUBLE VISION

The visual fields and images seen by the right eye are shown by vertical lines and those seen by the left eye by horizontal lines. Combined, they make up, in the central ellipsoid, the view of the world we normally see.

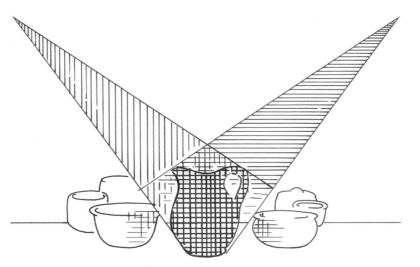

Despite the obvious advantages of two eyes, you can see quite adequately with one eye. Try closing one eye and looking at your clenched fist held in front of you, and then do the same closing the other eye. You get a somewhat different view of your fist with each eye, in what is called binocular parallax. But only with both eyes open will you also be able to see around your fist to any extent. You will find that depth and dimensions still are half-apparent with one eye, however, for these are partly calculated by the eye and brain working together.

HOW IT WORKS: points of view

AN ORIGINAL CYCLOPS

A scene from Homer's *Odyssey* is depicted on a Greek figure vase, in which Ulysses blinds a one-eyed cyclops. The word cyclops means literally "round eye".

YOU CAN SEE the value of binocular vision with a simple experiment. Hang a wire cube on cotton (*above*). If you look with both eyes, you see its cube shape. If you shut one eye, the shape looks more like a flat trapezoid than a cube. In fact, with one eye shut, your perception of depth becomes wildly inaccurate. Try catching a ball one-eyed, or getting a friend to drop a ball on a target on the floor. With two eyes, the difference between the views from each eye gives an accurate estimation of distance—the less the difference, the further away something is. With one eye, you can only judge by other clues.

IMAGE FUSION

The view from each eye can be quite different, and our brain fuses the separate images together to produce our view of the world around us. Strange things can happen if the image from one eye radically differs from that of the other, or the merging mechanism breaks down.

Although in the U.S., as in most countries, you drive on the right of the road, the dominance of the right eye in most people would theoretically suggest driving on the left, so that your dominant right eye can see the oncoming traffic better. In the days when horsemen ruled the road, it was the custom normally to ride on the left partly because of this.

For the images from each eye to fuse, their fields of view must match precisely. The match depends on the *fovea centralis*, a small depression in the back of the center of the retina. This contains only cone cells and is therefore the area of sharpest vision. If you are looking at an object more than about 20 feet (6 m) away, this matching can only come about if the eyes turn inward, or converge. The closer the object, of course, the more the eyes need to converge. At a certain point (very close indeed to your nose if you are nearsighted), you will no longer be able to focus with both eyes because they cross.

Image fusion normally takes place without you being remotely conscious of it. But significantly, your brain does not give equal weight to the images it receives from each eye. Just as you have a dominant hand and foot, so you have a dominant eye, which tends to be the right eye if you are righthanded. This is due to the way the brain is divided into two hemispheres. The dominant eye drives or determines your field of vision.

OPTICAL IMBALANCES

If image fusion fails, the result is double vision, an alarming state when the two images fail to combine. This may be due to drunkeness or the

effects of other drugs, brain injury or disease, or even food poisoning.

Strange things also happen when the images shown to each eye differ too radically from each other. The brain may first reject and then accept some parts of the image coming from each eye as it tries to form a single, solid picture. If the objects are of different colors, you may see first one color and then the other, rather than any combination of the two. If the patterns or contours are markedly different, separate parts of the images move in or out of your line of vision, changing and recombining in various ways. This is termed retinal or binocular rivalry. You can experience this phenomenon very easily by wearing a pair of three-dimensional glasses, with one red lens and the other green or blue. When you then look at patterns made up of the same two colors, you see the colors and forms separate bewilderingly.

VISUAL AID
A movie theater audience with special glasses to make screen images appear three-dimensional.

HOW IT WORKS:
dominant vision

YOU CAN DISCOVER for yourself which is your dominant eye by a simple experiment. Cut a tiny hole in the middle of a piece of ordinary white paper. Keeping both eyes open, hold the paper at arm's length towards a source of light, preferably artificial, and visually center the light in the hole. Then close each of your eyes, one at a time, and compare the visual fields. If you are righthanded, you will find that your left eye alone is way out of line for peeping through the hole!

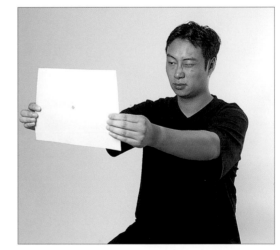

For another compelling demonstration of dominant vision, roll up a sheet of plain white paper and, while keeping both eyes open, hold the tube up to one eye with one hand. You should then gradually bring the palm of your other hand toward the tube until it is touching the outside of the tube near the end. You may be surprised by how far your dominant eye determines what you finally see with both your eyes.

STEREOSCOPES

Since the discovery of eyesight being stereoscopic in the 1800s, the interest in stereoscopes has faded in the early years of this century, with the coming of the movies. There was a revival in the early 1950s, and recently stereoscopy has been used in forgery detection and ballistics.

It took a surprisingly long time for Western artists and scientists to realize that human eyesight itself is stereoscopic. The term (from the Greek for solid sight) means related to seeing, or at least appearing to see, things in three dimensions. Only in 1755 did the British scientist Joseph Harris recognize the stereoscopic nature of our eyesight, writing: "And by the parallax on account of the distance betwixt our eyes, we can distinguish besides the front, part of the two sides of a near object...and this gives a visible relievo (relief) to such objects, which helps greatly to raise or detach them from the plane on which they lie." In other words, because we can move our two eyes, the resulting parallax enables us to see objects in all their three dimensions.

In 1833 the first crude stereoscope was developed by Charles Wheatstone (1802-75), a versatile English scientist and inventor who also invented the harmonica and concertina and an early form of the electric telegraph. His idea was wonderfully simple. He placed two pictures, one in front of each eye—each representing the viewpoint of a pair of eyes. To his surprise he discovered that plain line drawings, without any shading or other relief, stood out clearly and distinctly from their backgrounds, as though separated from it.

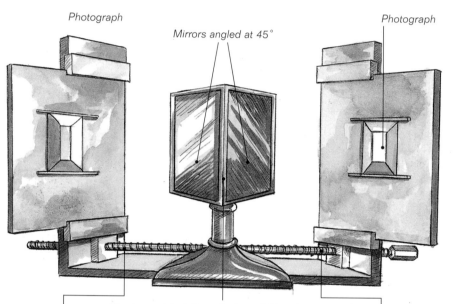

Photograph

Mirrors angled at 45°

Photograph

Viewing point—left eye looks at lefthand mirror and right eye looks at righthand mirror

Photographic mounts adjust closer or further away so photographs can be positioned properly in the two mirrors

HOW IT WORKS:

basic stereoscopes

YOU CAN MAKE a very simple stereoscope using only a pin and two identical pictures, although its effectiveness will depend on how closely your own eyes can converge. Hold up two small identical pictures (normal photographs will do) and take a pin in your other hand. As you bring the pin closer to your eyes, it should produce a very basic form of stereoscopic vision. This is tiring, however, and not very satisfactory even if your eyesight is sufficiently myopic (near sighted) to manage it, but it does illustrate the basic principles of stereoscopy.

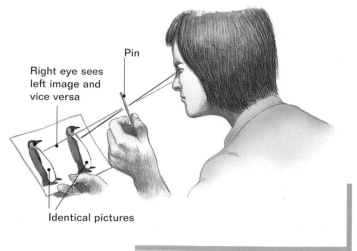

Pin

Right eye sees left image and vice versa

Identical pictures

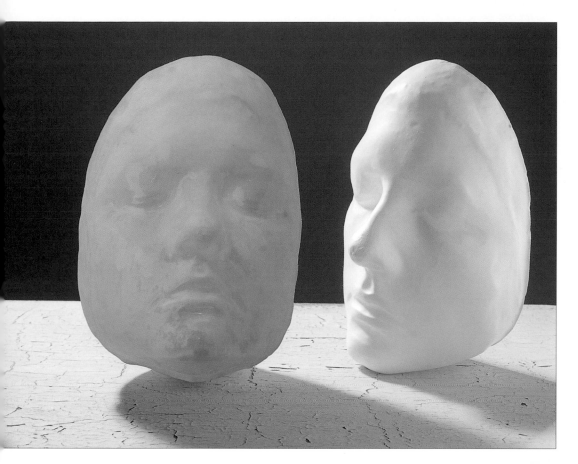

3-D DISGUISED

If you look into the inside of a mask—where it is hollowed out—and slowly rotate it from left to right, there is a certain point where instead of projecting inward, the features leap out towards you in a 3-D fashion.

However, Wheatstone realized that, for most people, looking at twin objects like this was visually too demanding, since there is a strong tendency for your eyes to converge on a central "fixation point." Moreover, the pictures had to be very small, since it is hard to adjust to objects much closer than 10 inches (25 cm) to your eyes. Wheatstone's solution was to devise a pair of mirrors, one in front of each eye, and angled at 45 degrees, reflecting pictures on either side. This allowed the viewer's vision to be fused.

In 1849, David Brewster developed a much better stereoscope, using lenses. The lenses were angled magnifying prisms. This meant the pictures could not only be smaller but also further apart than the eyes—yet still able to be fused. Brewster's instrument was smaller and more portable than Wheatstone's, and was ideal for photographs—the first successful photographic process dates from just ten years previously. Brewster's stereoscopes remained tremendously popular family entertainment for decades, showing people startling three-dimensional views, not only of comic scenes, but distant parts of the world, such as the pyramids of Egypt and the Victoria Falls.

Viewers soon found that if the right-eye picture is swapped with the left-eye picture, the impression of depth is often reversed. Solid things look hollow and hollow things solid. This is called pseudoscopic vision or false stereoscopy. Pseudoscopic vision does not always reverse depth, and this reveals something about our depth perception. You may not be able to see a pseudoscopic view of a statue in a hollow niche, for instance. Although the features of the statue should look hollow, they still appear to stand out. This is because your mind overrides what you actually see. A face is a face, says your unconscious mind, and a face has a nose and mouth sticking out, not hollowed in.

GROUP OF SCIENTISTS

From left to right—some of the great physicists and biologists of our time—Michael Faraday, T. H. Huxley, Sir Charles Wheatstone, Sir David Brewster, and John Tyndall.

HOLOGRAMS

Holograms are remarkable, apparently three-dimensional images made from nothing more substantial than light. You can look at them from different angles just as you can a solid object, yet they are made simply by the interference set up between a beam of laser light and its reflected and refracted counterpart.

The word hologram comes from the Greek *holos* meaning whole and *gram* or *graphy* meaning writing or message. Holography, like photography, is a technique for recording an object and then reproducing it on film—often standard photographic film.

Ordinary photographs record only the variations in brightness of the subject, giving only an illusion of depth and perspective (see Chapter 1). Holographs by contrast actually record the distance of different parts of the subject, so that they can give a true 3D image with real depth and perspective. They do this by using a laser beam as a reference light. A laser produces perfectly "coherent" light—that is, light in which all the waves are in step. It then reflects and refracts part of the beam off the subject so that waves come back slightly out of step with the reference beam. The holographic plate records these differences in phase. Since the difference in phase varies according to just how far from the plate a particular part of the subject is, the effect is to make a complete picture of the subject in three-dimensions. When the plate is developed to reconstruct the light pattern again, it gives a 3D image so convincing that you can experience motion parallax, the relative motion of two objects inside the hologram, as you walk around it (see Chapter 5).

Holography was originally conceived by Dennis Gabor, a Hungarian-born British scientist (1900–79). Gabor worked out the basic theory of holograms in 1947–48, but his ideas had to wait for nearly twenty years. The problem is that holograms will not work with ordinary light. Ordinary light is "incoherent"—that is, it contains a mix of light with waves out of step. So it would be impossible to record the phase changes created by the various distances to the subject. Holography had to wait until the development of the laser in the 1960s. Gabor finally won popular recognition when he received the Nobel Prize for Physics in 1971.

HOLOGRAM
Holograms can only be made in unnatural iridescent colors. But a good hologram can still stun with its remarkable presence. In the future it may be possible to stun cinema audiences with moving, full-colored holograms.

THE HOLOGRAM

A hologram is basically a negative or transparency much like an ordinary photograph. But it does not in any way resemble a photographic negative at all in close-up. Instead it is an unrecognizable chaos of stripes, whorls and rough fringes, called interference patterns.

These seemingly chaotic interference patterns, however, contain all the information necessary to recreate the hologram. When reilluminated at the correct angle by a laser beam similar to the original reference beam, the hologram scatters and rearranges the light waves into an exact three-dimensional representation of the object photographed. A three-dimensional virtual image of the whole object then becomes visible which, if you are looking on, appears to be behind the hologram.

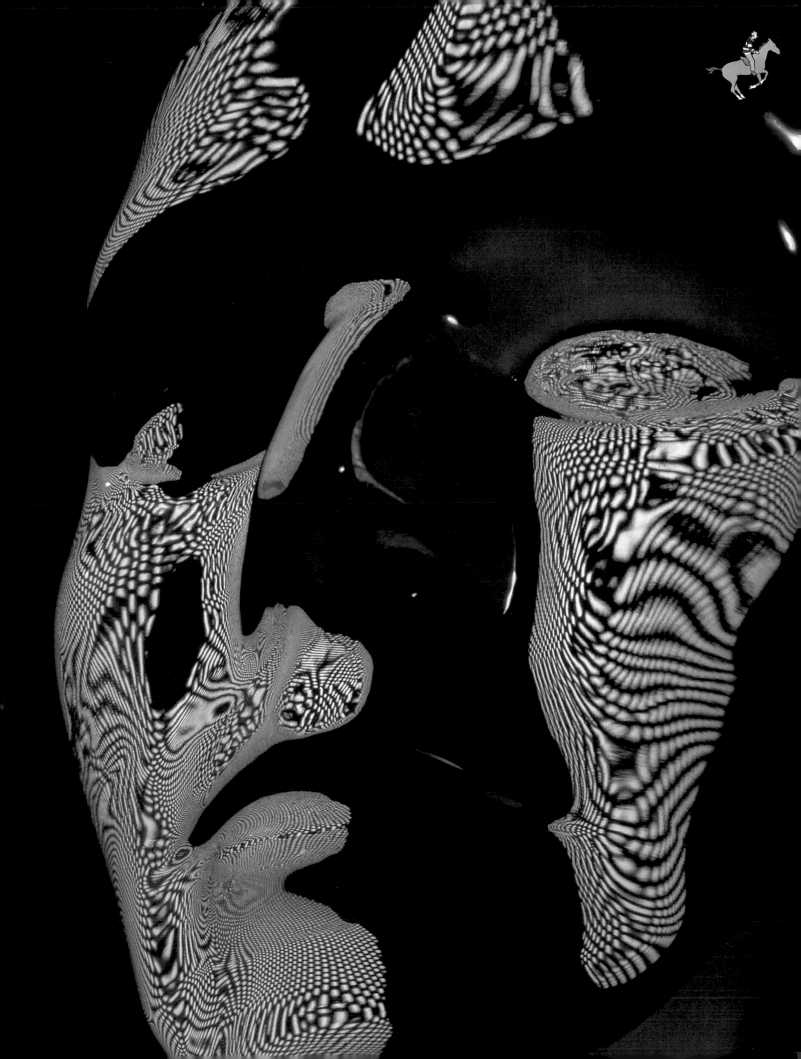

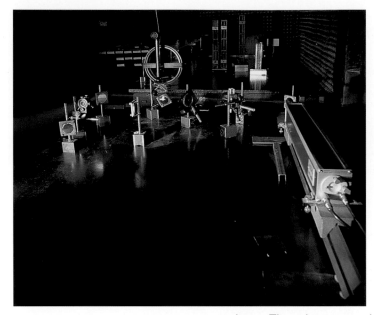

HOLOGRAPHIC CAMERA

The helium neon laser beam (*above*) moves around the holographic camera/table—weighing 2 tonnes to support all the equipment. Photographing a hologram requires a very long exposure—so the table also has dampers to ensure a steady shot without vibrations.

Viewed from the far side of the hologram, the complex reconstruction of the object can itself then be photographed as a three-dimensional object by normal cameras. From the near side a real image is also visible but only in fragments and this is often suppressed to avoid confusion and to enhance the main virtual image.

HOLOGRAMS IN ACTION

The most familiar use of holograms is probably on credit cards, where they are used as logos because they are so difficult, and expensive, to forge.

The holograms on credit cards are made by embossing. This is a mass-production process in which a hologram is recorded as a set of microscopic ripples onto a metal plate. The plate can then be used to transfer the pattern onto foil-backed film and used for printing magazines, record or book covers more cheaply than conventional methods.

Holograms are now found in fields as diverse as book covers, the nuclear electricity generating industry, jewelry and computers. A developing area of holography is in head-up displays (HDUs) in aircraft. These holograms reflect the light from the cockpit control display into the pilot's field of vision while still allowing him to see through the hologram to the world outside. This is particularly valuable in warplanes, where pilots rarely have time to look down at their instruments.

HOW IT WORKS: the hologram

1.The light from a laser is split into two beams.

2. A reference beam is reflected from a mirror over a slightly longer path.

3. Direct beam and reference beam are reflected from the subject out-of-step and so interfere with each other.

4. The interference pattern is recorded on a glass photographic plate.

5. When laser light is shone through the hologram at the same angle as the original reference beam, the light is scattered to project a 3D image.

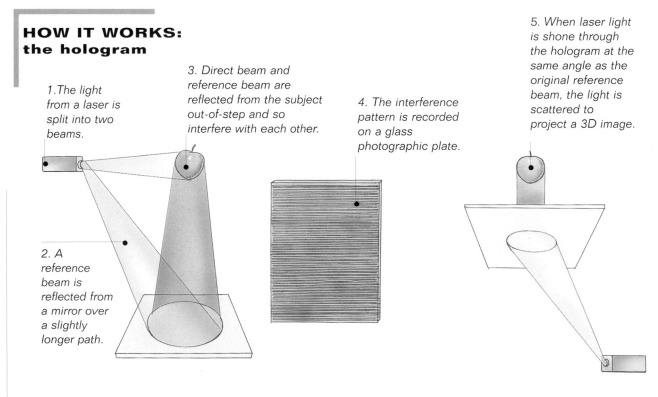

Precision is so important in these that they are made on a special holographic emulsion of "chromatic" ions rather than conventional photographic film.

In medicine too, holography is proving valuable. The concept of X-ray holography of biological cells is being developed and the medical possibilities of such three-dimensional views into the body are immense.

A distinctly more light-hearted use of holograms is in light shows, both as background decoration at parties or functions and as an art form in its own right. Increasing numbers of artists work with holography, often using computer-generated three-dimensional images that move.

HOLOGRAMS IN INDUSTRY

One of the bonuses of holography is that it can show up remarkably fine variations in structure—so fine that stress patterns show up in materials that look completely unaffected even under a microscope.

Holographic interferometry compares holograms of an object before and after a stress test, and so reveals any changes, however minute. For stress analysis in engineering, lasers called pulsed lasers are used to create holograms to examine the vibrations set up in a rapidly rotating turbine blade.

In the nuclear industry, radiation makes it much too dangerous to inspect fuel rods too closely. Instead, they make holograms of the rods, which can then be compared with holograms of the original rod to see if any minute cracks and defects have developed in between.

Probably the field with the greatest holographic potential, however, is in information storage and retrieval. Normal computer memories are sequential, with each separate item or bit of information linked to one memory. This makes the information very vulnerable if the central memory is damaged. But in a hologram each part of the image stores all of the information, so there is much less risk of total catastrophe. Multilaser computer chips are being developed that will retrieve holographic images from lithium niobate/gallium arsenide crystals capable of storing one trillion bits of information.

EAGLE

The illusion that the eagle opens its beak as the viewer moves round can be created by projecting two holograms taken from different angles.

left

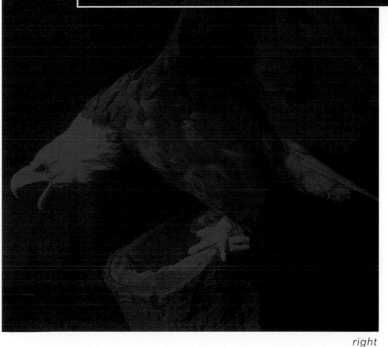

right

MAGIC EYE

The patterns on these pages appear to be flat areas of color without any particular sense or structure. But learn to focus on them in a particular way, and they will leap into three-dimensional life. They are autostereoscopes: images that can be seen in three dimensions without any extra equipment.

Lay the book completely flat. Move your eyes close to one of the images, until it becomes a blur. Relax into this blur until the shapes and patterns begin to separate and float into three dimensions. This may take a few minutes—don't panic! When you can hold onto the new image, slowly withdraw your head to about book reading distance. Adjust your eyes to let the image continue to gain in depth. If at first you don't succeed, rest for a while and try again. Alternatively turn to page 122-3.

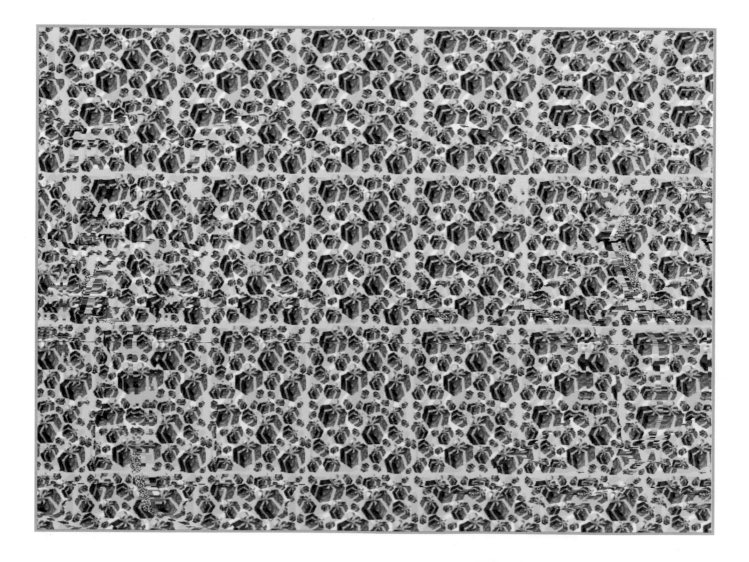

MAGIC EYE

103

CHAPTER 7
ILLUSORY FIGURES

Every time you see a landscape of almost any sort you can normally distinguish the foreground from the background and top from bottom. However, in 20:50 (left), at the Saatchi Gallery, London, Richard Wilson has used sump oil which, when completely still, reflects a perfect mirror image of whatever is opposite. This creates the illusion to the onlooker, when they walk out onto the black platform that they are standing on a walkway suspended a few feet above a structure that is the same as the glass ceiling. In reality, the ceiling is reflected in the sump oil, which rests at the same level as the platform—the optical illusion is so convincing that it is only by blowing on the oil and creating a ripple effect or by the smell of the oil that it is apparent this is an illusion.

ILLUSORY PERCEPTION

You do not see the world around quite as plainly and completely as you might think. Often the eye and brain, working together in a process still not completely understood, fill in or add detail to help you make sense of the visible world. The world you see is in fact full of "gaps" which you continuously ignore or compensate for.

You nearly always distinguish automatically between what appears to be the important "figure" in the foreground and the less important background, often on very arbitrary grounds. Objects which appear distinctly separate may not be so. Or objects may appear to run together when they are actually separate, which is the chief reason why camouflage works.

These simple visual illusions or "illusory figures" show your mind tripping a wire or coming to false conclusions. Such illusions occur because images formed on the retina of the eye in fact make up only patterns of light and dark. You are able to decipher them into meaningful images only through memories of what other, broadly similar, objects were like.

BRIDGING THE GAP

We may talk about seeing things "right in front of our noses" but this is the one area which we definitely cannot see. To prove it, take a broken image such as the hands (*above right*), and bring it close to your nose. At a certain point the separate images converge. Your eyes, no longer able to accommodate at such a close range, have wrongly deduced that there is no gap.

There are many instances of ground and figure confusion in people of all cultures. The Danish psychologist Edgar Rubin investigated such figure-ground reversals with a series of wittily contrived drawings. In one, rather grotesque example that he gives (*right*), you imagine you can see a face with a long nose and leering mouth against a dark ground—but equally, the black, lefthand side of the picture could easily be something set against a white ground. The two figures in Rubin's sketch "compete" with each other for your attention, each, in effect, trying to establish its visual dominance.

Another example of this competition of figures and grounds comes in Rubin's radial cross. Here, the ambiguity depends mainly on which equally compelling image is seen first: the concentric cross (which alternatively appears as a series of concentric circles) or the radial cross (which alternatively appears as a circle of radial lines). In each case, the lines of what is seen as the ground appear to continue behind what is seen as the figure, although it is tantalizingly ambiguous.

MERGING INTO THE BACKGROUND

The leopard's spots (*above*) merge with dappled light and dark, creating a camouflage effect which confuses any passing eye.

MAKING CONTACT

Draw the image (*above*) closer and closer to your nose. At a certain point the fingers will touch, as your eyes are not able to accommodate such close-range vision.

REVERSED OUT

Look twice at this Edgar Rubin reversible figure—a profile of a face, or a supplicating figure?

HOW IT WORKS:

illusory figure

YOU CAN CREATE an experimental illusory figure yourself very easily (*below*). Simply draw a series of intersecting straight lines on a piece of white paperboard, making a crude star shape, and then erase the center. This creates a small white disc. The inner ends of the lines now appear to be connected by a ghostly circle, like a sun—a totally illusory, but visually quite convincing contour.

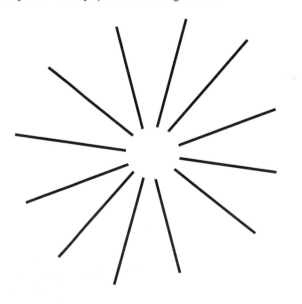

FIGURE AND GROUND

We could not move around safely without distinguishing foreground from background. But sometimes figure and ground can be swapped around with remarkable ease.

Wang Jia Nan

STANDING ON TOP OF THE MOUNTAIN

Unusually in an oriental painting, a figure provides a sense of scale in an imposing landscape.

Every time you look at a picture of almost any sort—a painting, a photograph or even a moving picture in a film—you automatically distinguish the vitally important figure in the foreground from the far less important background or ground. This may nonetheless include minor human or other figures as well as inanimate objects. Such unconscious prejudgments have been built into the Western way of seeing the world, at least since the Renaissance. But this hierarchical grading or distinction is not the only way things can be. It is possible, sometimes even inevitable, that figure and ground may reverse, producing effects which are intriguing, even alarming.

One of the oldest and still most potent examples of the reversal of ground and figure is the Chinese Yin/Yang symbol. In the Yin/Yang sign figure and ground are inextricably bound up together, the shape of one creating the other, each containing the germ of its opposite. Here it is impossible to say which is figure and which is ground. This famous symbol illustrates the ancient Chinese belief in the complementary harmony of Yin (the female cosmic principle, dark, passive, cool and moist) and Yang (the male principle: active, fiery, hot and dry), which govern all life in its myriad transformations. The pattern of transformation, which include the cyclical reversal of male and female, is called the Tao (the Way). The often deeply mystical Chinese religion and philosophy called Taoism took such an interwoven emblem as its symbol of the interdependability of opposites, and humans and their surroundings. East Asian art (Chinese, Japanese and Korean) in fact makes far less rigid distinctions between figure and ground. In typical Oriental paintings, not only is there no linear perspective, with houses and people the same size higher up the picture in the distance as they are at the bottom. There are also empty spaces in the picture that have almost as much importance and weight as the drawn figures. Such ambiguity about ground and figure would be almost unthinkable in a traditional formal western landscape but is readily accepted by East Asian traditions.

ALTERNATIVE FOCUS

The ancient Tao symbol (*above*) exemplifies the complementary dual nature of the universe (male and female, active and passive). It also graphically illustrates how figure and ground can be easily reversed.

SIZING UP

Our eyes have to make judgments about relative size. The tiny man (*right*) about to be crushed looks like a dwarf. Or is he normal, and the man holding him a giant?

LIGHT AND DARK

Without light you cannot see at all, which is one reason why your eyes turn towards things that are brightly lit. But your eyes can become baffled, over-stimulated by light, and "remember" light long after it has ceased to shine.

One reason that your eye is so easily baffled by figures like Rubin's is that it is drawn towards light. So it focuses on figures and forms that are bright rather than those that are dark. Bright figures inherently appear larger and stronger than dark ones, although they may be identically sized. The sun appears much larger than the moon in the sky when seen at the same angle because it is much brighter —even though the discs are a similar size. Illusions like these arise because, when a strong light reaches your retina, it stimulates not only the receptors directly struck by light but also those around it. These receptor cells are grouped in "batteries." Proportionately more cells react to a bright object than to a dark one of identical size. When you look at a bright figure against a dark ground, some of your receptors in neighboring dark regions of the retina are also aroused. This gives you the impression of seeing something as larger than it actually is. The reverse happens when you see a dark figure against a bright ground, which is why dark sculptures intended to stand against a light background are often made larger than they would otherwise be.

SUN AND MOON

By remarkable coincidence, the discs of the Sun and the Moon actually appear the same size in the sky—because although the Sun is 400 times as wide as the Moon, it is also 400 times as far away. When, rarely, both are seen in the sky at the same time, the Sun appears much bigger because it is much brighter.

SEEING STARS

Look at the drawings of the two stars. At first glance, the white stars in the lefthand picture look slightly larger than the black stars in the righthand picture. In fact, all the stars are identical in size as well as shape, but your eye very slightly enlarges a bright figure against a dark ground. The stars in the real night sky are even smaller than they look.

HOW IT WORKS:

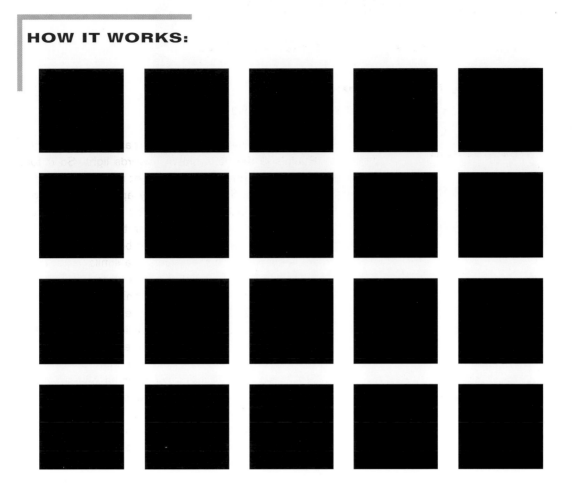

Another example of this bright/dark confusion comes when looking at the honeycomb of white discs (below right). The white dots almost block out the black interstices when you view it from any distance or even with your eyes unfocused. Similarly, when looking at the so-called Hermann Grid Illusion (see above) you will find that the white bands appear extremely white. More intriguingly, if you look long enough at the grid, gray spots will appear at the intersections. The reasons for these spots are not fully understood, but it has been suggested that the white at the intersections has less competition from the black squares, and so looks less pristinely white than the uncluttered lines themselves.

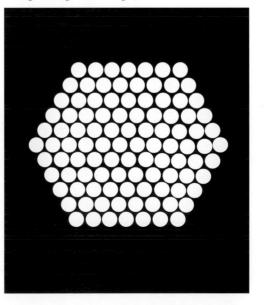

RELATIVITY

Earlier this century, in his twin theories of relativity—Special and General—the scientific genius Albert Einstein (1879-1955) created a vision of time and space that has completely shattered our common sense way of looking at the world—and suggested that in some ways our entire perception is an illusion.

Einstein's theories completely overturned our down-to-earth notions of space and time. In his special theory, Einstein showed that time and space were relative, not absolute. The passage of time—or the speed of an object—is not fixed but can be measured only by comparison. Time and distance can expand or shrink according to where you measure them from. In his general theory, Einstein showed how gravity can actually bend space—so that even a straight line is not an absolute.

In the face of this assault upon our common sense, our faith in what we see should be—and has been—profoundly shaken. On a simple level, it reminds us of day-to-day illusions. Common sense tells us the Earth is perfectly still, and the Sun and stars glide by through the heavens. Even though we know this is not true, our every sense fights against the notion. And if this is true on such a fundamental, gigantic way, in how many other ways are we deceived? The possibility that there may be many, many more dimensions to reality than our eyes tell us has both haunted and inspired many artists this century. Of one image, Escher writes "three gravitational forces operate perpendicular to one another. Men are walking in crisscrosses on the floor and the stairs. Some of them, though belonging to different worlds, come very close together but can't be aware of one another's existence." A chillingly lonely vision of a post-Einstein universe.

DID YOU KNOW?

Relative size

PERSPECTIVE IS IN MANY ways a complete illusion. Absolute mathematical, linear, or scientific perspective is only a Western artefact, no more than 600 years old at most. In reality, the way we see the world is far more relative. This picture is a powerful illustration of this. Look at the two groups of circles. In the bottom one, the center circle will strike you as distinctly small. If you then look at the circle at the top, the central circle will appear larger, but if you actually measure it, you will find it is exactly the same size as its brother below. Perceptions of size are relative and depend crucially on their context.

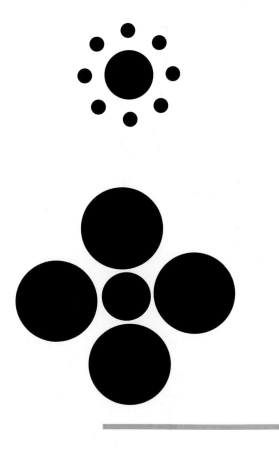

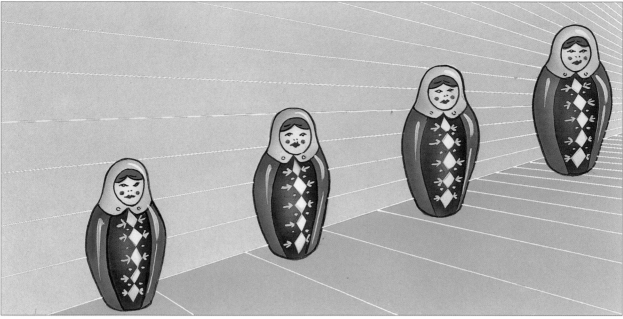

HOW IT WORKS:

mirage

ONE FORM OF VISUAL illusion has been the subject of many legends, often connected with sailors lost at sea or people dying of thirst in deserts. Mirages, however, have an objective existence, and are caused by certain combinations of light and temperature, normally but not invariably at sea or in deserts. You can also experience them looking along a highway in hot weather, when the air shimmers above the hot asphalt and creates visual illusions. The expansion of the super-heated air causes light waves passing through it to bend and create almost a mirror-effect. Among the most spectacular of mirages is that sometimes observed in the Straits of Messina between the toe of Italy and Sicily.

Very peculiar local atmospheric conditions create inverted reflections of ships, mountains, and even cities often many miles from the real object, which seem to float in the sky like fantasies. With travelers dying of heat and thirst in the Sahara, however, a psychological element of wishful thinking certainly enters into the image of delectable oases shaded by palm trees.

THE CAMERA OFTEN LIES

The photograph seems so real and so impartial, that we are far more easily fooled into thinking that what a photograph shows is true and accurate than we ever would be with a painting. But even before the days of computer manipulation and morphing, the camera could, and did, often lie.

DISAPPEARING FIGURES

One of the simplest and most effective ways the camera can be made to lie is by removing unwanted detail. This might simply be an unsightly shadow, wrinkle or spot— easily removed in the darkroom or on screen, by retouching —but the removal may also be something far more sinister...

CZECHED OUT

CZECH PRIME MINISTER Alexander Dubcek was "rubbed out" by the Soviet regime during the doomed Prague Spring of 1968. The first, genuine, photograph (top right) shows Dubcek with President Svoboda in front of Prague Cathedral. In the second photograph (right), released after the Soviets had crushed his attempts at reform, he has mysteriously vanished. A photographic retoucher bleached Dubcek out of the picture and carefully printed into the bleached out area a new photo of the background buildings. The retoucher was careless, however— one of Dubcek's feet can still be seen!

MIXED MESSAGES

PHOTOMONTAGE HAS always been significant, and with the advent of computer manipulation, it has become absolutely massive, and probably the most extensively used kind of illusion of all—adverts, films, posters, and works of art such as The Lia Fáil of Waterford (left) collage by Seán Hillen, all use photomontage to show anything from a man cavorting on the moon to giant dinosaurs bearing down on minute humans.

SCHOOL CLONE

ONE FINE-OLD FASHIONED photographic illusion came from the traditional school photo, when hundreds of students and staff lined up together to be photographed. Because a wide-angle lens would produce massive distortion, the photographer got the group in by taking several separate shots, panning down the line between shots, and then assembling them for the final print. As seen in this photograph (left), a quick and mischievous student could run from one end of the group to the other between shots and so appear twice in the same photograph.

VISUAL AFTER-EFFECTS

Some types of optical illusion are not tricks of the mind. They involve your mind only marginally, if at all. The most common of these illusions of the eye are visual after-effects—the tendency for images to persist in the eye after you have stopped looking at them. Everybody experiences these at times, but there is remarkably little scientific agreement over what is their exact cause.

After you are photographed with even a moderately powerful flashbulb, you often see a dark blob in the middle of your field of vision. Filmstars facing the massed photographers of the press may face such a barrage of flash that they can be half-blinded for some time. The reason for this blob is that the photoreceptors in your eye have become fatigued or, rather they have adapted to this intense light stimulation.

Similarly, if a dark room is suddenly illuminated by a bright light, you may see the whole room lit up for some moments afterward in what is called "eidetic imagery". After the light stimulus has stopped, the nerve fibers in the retina of your eye continue to generate signals for a fraction of a second afterwards. This is retinal lag—a process performed by the eye central to the illusion of moving pictures (*see pp 82-3*).

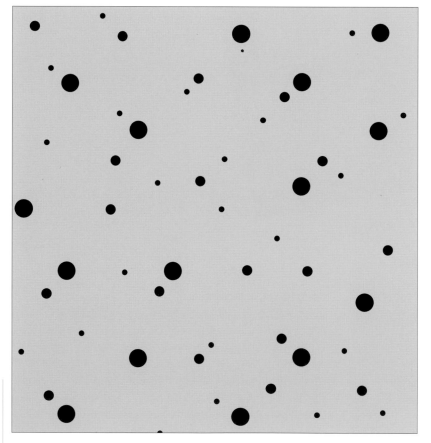

HOW IT WORKS: after images

THERE IS NO NEED TO start taking flash photographs to experience an after image. You can do so with your own television. Simply turn the television on, look at the image for a while and then immediately look at a blank wall. You will probably notice a faint but definite after image of whatever has been on the television screen still showing against the wall. In fact, you experience this effect so frequently that you normally just disregard it.

OP ART
Look at the image (above), based on Bridget Riley's *Fragment No. 6*, and after 30 seconds you will see white circles dancing among the black ones as the eye becomes tired—Bridget Riley, one of the best known 'Op Artists' of the 1960s, exploited the tendency of the eye to become fatigued with excess stimulus in her bedazzling pictures.

NEGATIVE IMAGES

The reason for after images is little under-stood, but this is what is thought to happen. If after a flash there is no further stimulus, the photoreceptors return to their resting state after a period of retinal lag. While they are doing so, you may experience another after image. This is caused by the photoreceptors reaction to normal, gentle light. The effect is to create exactly the opposite effect of a brilliant light: the dark spot or other image which persists for a while in the middle of your field of vision. This "negative" after image often seems immense, blotting out a large portion of your visual field, because it still occupies a large portion of your retina, no matter how far off the objects you are looking at afterwards.

Such "negative persistence" can often be experienced even with very simple, quite dull images. You may see a negative after image when your eye is half confused by changes in the surroundings of a simple object on which you have been concentrating. If you stare at a printed image of a simple black shape for about 30 seconds, for instance, then shift your gaze across to a white section of the page, you will probably see a ghostly after image of the shape.

Such negative after images can happen with colors too. If you look intently for a half a minute or more at a simple picture with just one color, then shift your gaze to white paper, you will see a ghostly after image in color. But the color you see is not the same color as before; instead it is its complementary color, its exact opposite on a color wheel. In other words, you see a negative color, just as you see negative bright-ness after a flash.

CAGED PARROT
Stare at the red bird for 30 seconds in bright light. Now look at the center of the bird cage on the left. You should then see an illusory green bird in the cage.

DID YOU KNOW?
how electric
lights work

ORDINARY ELECTRIC LIGHT BULBS actually flare up and down 60 times per second because the electric current alternates. But the light looks continuous because of retinal lag. At this speed, the light flares up again while the previous bright flare still persists in the eye. Fluorescent lights, however, often have a slower flash cycle rate so may appear to flicker when seen out of the corner of your eye. But if you look directly at a fluorescent tube, the flickering disappears. The reason for this is that images in the corner of your eye are seen mainly with rods, which have only a brief retinal lag. Images in the center of your eye are seen with cones as well, which have a longer lag.

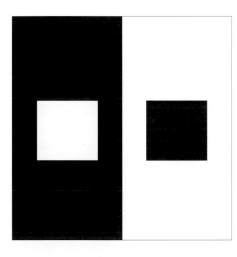

SQUARE EYES
Look at the black square in a white rectangle (*right*) speedily for a minute or so. Then look at the black area to its left. The brilliant contrast of white against black may persist even though you are no longer looking at the black square. Blinking may even bring it back.

The exact cause of these color after images has not been firmly established. It is thought that they occur as the cones—the photore-ceptors in your eye sensitive to colors—become fatigued, or saturated with light, or simply over–adapting to intense light. Scientists have even suggested a temporary 'bleaching' of the photopigments in the cones of your eye. Another idea is that it may be due to general fatigue of the nervous system which organizes and transmits stimuli to your brain.

PHOTOGRAPHIC MEMORY

Each new visual input is temporarily stored in the brain before gradually fading. Sometimes, a stored image can be a valuable photographic memory. Sometimes it lingers on to create illusions.

FAST TRACK

When driving, we rely on surroundings to give a clue to speed. But these can be misleading. The closeness of the bridge girders here might normally give an illusion of speed—but it may depend on how fast you were traveling before. After a long, fast drive on the highway, your brain may have adjusted to things passing by quickly—and fool you into thinking you are now moving very slowly.

One aspect of after images which has proved particularly fascinating is eidetic imagery or photographic memory. Most after images are vague and fade away after a few moments, but eidetic images are unusually vivid and sharply defined. They may persist undimmed in the memory for many minutes.

Some people can hold an eidetic after image clear in their mind and examine it, counting the number of cups on a table, for example. For those who can so hold on to eidetic images, it is normally only necessary to look at the original picture for a few seconds to have it imprinted on their visual memory. This is an unconscious process, however, for it has been found that actively attempting to concentrate on parts of the image causes it to break up or fade away very swiftly.

Some research suggests that up to five per cent of American school children have an eidetic ability, and the figure may be even higher in other cultures.

MOTION

The visual after-effects described so far depend on the world being stationary, but there are also important after-effects of moving images. One obvious after-effect is the distortion of perceived speed when, after travelling fast on a freeway, you come off it onto a slower road in an urban environment. A speed of 30 mph (50 km/h) may seem almost a walking

pace by comparison, as your eye is still attuned to the speed of the faster freeway traffic.

Another example of motion after-effects becomes obvious when experimenting with a spiral. Cut out a spiral like the one illustrated (*right*) and spin it clockwise. It will appear to expand. After you have watched it for a few seconds, stop it and observe the visual after-effects. It will appear to shrink quite markedly, although of course it is still the same size throughout. Your eye has been baffled by the rotating spiral.

BLIND SPOT

Similar to visual effects is your blind spot, the gap in the middle of your vision. This occurs because there are no receptors in front of the optic nerve at the back of the retina. Normally you fail to notice this because an area covered by the blind spot of one eye is covered by the photoreceptors of the other, but there are occasions when both eyes fail you. This hole in our visual field was discovered only in 1668 by the French scientist Edme Mariotte (1620–1684), who caused a sensation by demonstrating it at the court of Charles II of England in 1668. He astonished the court by making things vanish when they corresponded with the blind spot.

SPINNING OUT

The eye and brain constantly try to make sense of the world—and in doing so fall into traps. With these spiral tops, the brain adjusts to the motion and sees the spiral bands as bigger than they are. When you stop the top, the brain clings on to this adjustment, and so believes the bands have shrunk.

HOW IT WORKS: the blind spot

YOU CAN TEST this yourself by looking at the illustration of two playing cards (*below*). Cover your right eye and look at the eight of spades card. When the eight of spades is about 16 inches from your eye, the king of spades on the left will vanish. The band will appear a uniform black, just as it would appear red or green if it were red or green, for your brain has filled in the gap.

UNFAMILIAR FACES

The differences between human faces are remarkably small, yet we can recognize familiar faces instantly. But what if those faces are subtly altered or presented in a different way?

MAN OF MYSTERY

Often people being interviewed on television wish to disguise their identity for one reason or other. Television engineers oblige them by "pixellating" the area of the picture where their face appears. Every part of the television picture is captured on pixels, individual light-sensitive electronic cells which simply register the intensity of light falling on them. These are so small that we don't usually see them individually. Pixellation means grouping them into blocks, so that we see them as squares of different light intensity. The bigger the blocks, the harder the picture becomes to recognize. This heavily pixellated image is of someone who would not wish to remain anonymous. Can you guess who? Turn to pp.122-3 for the answer.

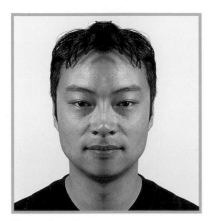

Two right sides

Normal

Two left sides

TWO-FACED?

People's faces are always slightly asymmetrical, and that is how we expect them to be. We always like to think we have a good side and a bad side—but put two of your good sides together and they look just as bizarre as two bad sides as the series above shows. To try this out for yourself, stick a sheet of new foil very evenly and tightly on to a square of thin card. Place the foil card vertically on the dotted line in the portrait (*right*). Look at the face reflected first on the left (two left halves), then on the right (two right halves). They look like completely different people. In fact, you might even find it difficult to recognize someone transformed like this. You can do the same on yourself with the foil card and a photo of yourself, or even in front of a mirror.

ANSWERS

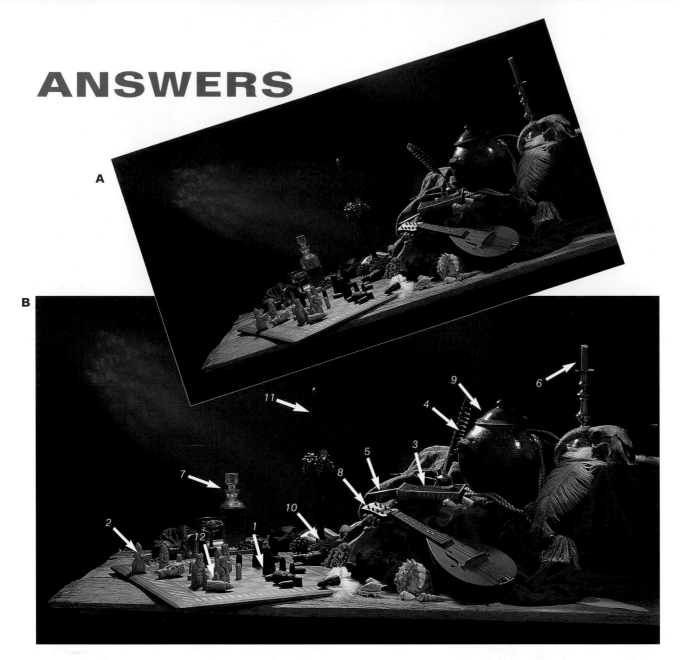

PAGES 1-2 SPOT THE DIFFERENCE— BETWEEN A. AND B.

IN PHOTOGRAPH B:

1. A black pawn has been removed from the chessboard.
2. A white knight sitting on the edge of the board has moved further left.
3. The shell on the book has disappeared.
4. The feather in the ink well has been turned and is now further to the right.
5. The feather bookmark has been lifted.
6. The candle on the right has burnt down lower and is now shorter than in *A*.

7. There's surprisingly more wine in the decanter!
8. The mandolin has been tuned because its keys are now in different positions.
9. The lid of the pottery jar is now slightly askew.
10. One of the two fir cones by the candlestick in the center has disappeared.
11. What was a blue candle in the center is now a red one.
12. A white pawn by the white king has been removed from the chessboard.

PAGE 39 *(above)*
There are 20 black and cream tools in total.

A

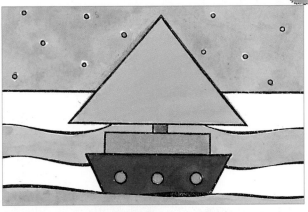

B

PAGES 46-47 *(above and right)*
Painted in different colors, what did look like a girl's face peering through a letterbox becomes a fish tank in A. Swimming around the plants and seaweed (formerly the girl's hair) are two fish which used to be the girl's eyes. Also, what was a blue boat with white sails on page 47, becomes a green Christmas tree in a red bucket in B above.

PAGE 102 *(above)*
Surprise! The magic eye shows a heart-shaped gift in a ribboned box which has just been unwrapped.

PAGE 103 *(above)*
The magic eye shows a wolf howling to the moon.

PAGE 120 *(left)*
The man of mystery is Abraham Lincoln, (1809-65), sixteenth President of the United States (1861-65).

INDEX

CREDITS

Key: a above, b below,
c centre, l left, r right

Ace Photo Agency
85b, 99, 100, 101a, 101b

AKG London
12, 15, 18bl, 19ar, 25r, 26, 28,
58, 71a, 72al, 75, 78a, 80al,
81ar, 82, 83

Cordon Art, Baarn,
Netherlands
43, 65a, 66, 67, 68a, 69

**Davies Keeling
Trowbridge Ltd**, *London*
8, 24r

Bruno Ernst
70a

E.T. Archive
11, 44, 53, 81b, 93

Shigeo Fukuda
68b

Frontline Art Publishing,
USA 102, 103

Getty Images
17a, 57, 94, 95a, 97b, 120

Giraudon
6, 24l, 25l, 45al

Tim Hawkins
98

J.D. Hillberry
1

Seán Hillen
115a

The Image Bank
110a, 112b

Imperial War Museum
42

David King Collection
114a, 114c

La Belle Aurore
37al

**Martin Mossop/Sunday
Times Style Section**
59

National Gallery, *London*
21, 22, 23l, 23r, 56

National Portrait Gallery,
London
55

Papilio Photographic
89

**Peter Newark's Historical
Pictures**
37br, 88b

Professor Penrose
64b, 65b

Pictor International
18al, 35, 78b, 80b, 106, 118

Saatchi Collection,
London/Richard Wilson
104

Sandro del Prete
45br, 70b

Shout Pictures
36br

*'Take A Close Look' written
and illustrated by*
Keith Kay, *1989*
40l, 40b, 40r, 41a, 41r, 41b,
88a, 107b

Visual Arts Library
86

The Stationary Office,
Norwich
36l, 36ar

*The photograph on page 114
appears courtesy of Sally Bond*

*We would also like to thank
Professor Richard Gregory for
the use of his artworks which
originally appeared in his book
'The Intelligent Eye'.*